Praise for *Am I Safe Here?*

"Short's compelling book contributes to the increasing awareness that
the notion of a 'safe school' needs to move beyond policies, programs,
security measures, and responses to individual incidents. Short weaves
direct, powerful quotes from the students throughout his book, thereby
empowering them to share their experiences, expertise, and insights.
The students' comments combined with his sound recommendations
provide direction for meaningful, sustainable change. It is the respon-
sibility of all educators to hear their voices, ultimately assuring LGBTQ
students: 'Yes. You are safe here.'"

> – MARY HALL, PHD, DIRECTOR OF SAFE SCHOOLS MANITOBA

"Am I Safe Here? is an essential resource for administrators and teachers
at both elementary and secondary schools. The systemic approach that
calls for cultural change in developing an LGBTQ-positive school setting
in all grades and in all spaces surpasses the limiting incident-based
reactionary approach. School administrators and teachers now have a
meaningful tool to address heterosexism and cisgenderism and to create
LGBTQ-inclusive schools for students, teachers, and staff."

> – NICK MULÉ, PHD, FOUNDER, QUEER ONTARIO

"An important read for folks interested in ending homophobic/
transphobic bullying and including LGBTQ students in full citizenship in
our school settings."

> – SUSAN RUZIC, ASSISTANT DIRECTOR OF SOCIAL JUSTICE, PROFESSIONAL
> AND SOCIAL ISSUES DEPARTMENT, BC TEACHERS' FEDERATION

"If you're looking for another book full of academic theory and sad statistics about the experiences of LGBTQ youth in schools, this isn't the book for you. Short brilliantly positions LGBTQ youth as the experts on their own experiences. He demonstrates how these students have become the educators on LGBTQ issues in their schools, which begs the question: Where are the teachers and what are they doing? LGBTQ youth shouldn't be the only ones advocating for change. In fact, they have the most to risk.

"Short provocatively blends together the first-hand experiences of LGBTQ youth to focus on a model to create equity-seeking schools that are supported by comprehensive LGBTQ policies, inclusive curriculum, visible and "out" LGBTQ teachers, gay-straight alliances, ongoing professional development, and proactive school administrators as key ingredients in challenging and changing a toxic heteronormative school culture. Make no mistake: there is a revolution happening in our schools. Classrooms are the battleground. And our LGBTQ students are the ones leading the way."

– KRISTOPHER WELLS, ASSISTANT PROFESSOR AND FACULTY DIRECTOR, INSTITUTE FOR SEXUAL MINORITY STUDIES AND SERVICES, FACULTY OF EDUCATION, UNIVERSITY OF ALBERTA

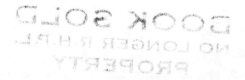

AM I SAFE HERE?

DONN SHORT

AM I SAFE HERE?

LGBTQ TEENS AND BULLYING IN SCHOOLS

on point PRESS | a UBC Press imprint
Vancouver . Toronto

26 25 24 23 22 21 20 19 18 17   5 4 3 2 1

Printed in Canada on FSC-certified ancient-forest-free paper
(100% post-consumer recycled) that is processed chlorine- and acid-free.

Library and Archives Canada Cataloguing in Publication

Short, Donn, author
Am I safe here? : LGBTQ teens and bullying in schools / Donn Short.

Includes bibliographical references.
Issued in print and electronic formats.
ISBN 978-0-7748-9020-5 (hardcover).–ISBN 978-0-7748-9021-2 (softcover).–
ISBN 978-0-7748-9022-9 (PDF).–ISBN 978-0-7748-9023-6 (EPUB).–
ISBN 978-0-7748-9024-3 (Kindle)

1. Lesbian students – Canada. 2. Gay students – Canada. 3. Bisexual students –
Canada. 4. Transgender youth – Canada. 5. Sexual minorities – Canada.
6. Teenagers – Canada. 7. Bullying in schools – Canada. I. Title.

LC2576.C3S56 2017   371.826'60971   C2017-903621-1
                                                   C2017-903622-X

Canadä

UBC Press, which owns the On Point Press imprint,
gratefully acknowledges the financial support for our publishing program
of the Government of Canada (through the Canada Book Fund),
the Canada Council for the Arts, and the British Columbia Arts Council.

Printed and bound in Canada by Marquis
Set in Calibri, Helvetica Condensed, and Sabon
by Artegraphica Design Co. Ltd.

On Point Press, an imprint of UBC Press
The University of British Columbia
2029 West Mall
Vancouver, BC V6T 1Z2
www.ubcpress.ca

For Keith and Corey

It's just, when you're walking down the hall, you hear,
"Oh, that's so gay, dude" or "He's such a fag." My friend
Robert is the only one in the school who's really out, and so
if he walks by, you might hear some people say, "Oh yeah,
that guy's such a fag." No one ever says anything to his face.
No one says anything about him being gay to his face. You
know what you can get away with and what you can't. I
mean, not officially, not what the school says, but you can.
It's more complex than that. Yeah. It's a greater complexity,
you know? You gotta change everything.

– KATIE, GRADE 12 STUDENT, TORONTO

Contents

Preface

"Pick a point and enter," she said.

Good advice, I thought. The speaker at the front of the room was giving advice on how to start a project that needed starting. So I picked a point. I had been thinking for some time about LGBTQ students in schools: How could I help? What needed to be done? What was there to do that wasn't already being done?

At the same time, many schools, teachers, and parents in Ontario were engaging in some very heavy conversations about "making schools safe" in the province. I had just arrived in Toronto from Vancouver and had not really paid much attention to Ontario's *Safe Schools Act*, which seemed to be the focus of a lot of the conversations.

The Safe Schools Act, passed in 2000, was really a bill amending Ontario's Education Act, but it was always referred to as a discrete piece of legislation. The first thing I looked for was a definition of *safety* in the act. The first thing I noticed was that there wasn't one. So that was my point of entry.

What did *safety* mean? Who got to define *safety*? How had the legislature and the public talked about safety before the bill's passage? And although school safety is an issue for all students, I was interested specifically in LGBTQ students. What did *safety* mean to LGBTQ students? How did they define *safety*, and how did that compare with what their schools were doing?

Reading through newspaper and media accounts, I saw that the Safe Schools Act was in many ways a product of the zero-tolerance discussions surrounding extreme school violence of the 1990s. The influence of the school shootings in Columbine, Colorado, and at W.R. Myers High School in Taber, Alberta, was evident.

In Ontario, the first serious steps toward implementing a zero-tolerance approach to school safety began in the early 1990s, with public demands for increased "discipline" in schools as a result of a series of violent incidents in a number of Toronto high schools, particularly some incidents with knives at schools in Scarborough.

Not surprisingly, in response to media and parental demands for solutions to school violence, politicians, school administrators, and others viewed safety in terms of zero-tolerance policies, expulsion, suspension, security guards, surveillance cameras, and punishment after the fact.

At the same time as this "hunker down" approach was taking root, however, there had also been an almost thirty-year journey in Toronto schools toward equity. Although the "fortress" mentality seems to me to leave the particular safety of LGBTQ students out of the safety equation, the efforts to bring "equity" to Toronto schools have put LGBTQ concerns front and centre.

Many administrators, teachers, and others contributed to this decades-long effort. Toronto District School Board equity officer Tim McCaskell was one of the leading figures. I knew I had to talk with him. He was very helpful, the best possible real-world entry point. He introduced me to a number of teachers who were stressing equity in their classrooms in order to help LGBTQ students feel welcome, included, and safe.

The first teacher I spoke to suggested another teacher. And she another. And so on and so on. I relied on this network of teachers committed to equity. From the start, I became aware of how much great work was being done in Toronto schools – by administrators, teachers, and students themselves.

I spent many weeks observing, listening to, and talking with the people I met – mainly students. This book represents the results of that time. I couldn't believe how much work was being done to make schools equitable and safe. I never ceased to be amazed at the depth of knowledge the students possessed and at the very smart and informed opinions and ideas I was hearing. That was a relief. I had worried that maybe no one would have anything to say.

They had some ideas that most would think of as dangerous to the status quo of schools. But that was their point. *Transform the schools,* they told me. *Rethink everything.* Well, as Oscar Wilde said, an idea that is not dangerous is not worthy of being called an idea.

Each day was exhilarating. Even the time I was called a fag by a student, one of the school's self-appointed guardians on the lookout for my type, had its positive aspect bound up in the sting. I was coming to understand the matter-of-factness of what was going on and beginning to appreciate that there was something that could be done about it.

I started out with my attention on bullying but came away at the end understanding that the students themselves saw the threat to their safety as much broader than that. They talked about heterosexism, heteronormativity, invisibility, and inclusiveness. How did they know all that?

At its core, this book is about seven different schools in the Toronto area and the people I met there. But you will also hear from teachers, administrators, and people in other locations such as Vancouver, Edmonton, and Thunder Bay.

The names of the schools have been changed, as have the names of the individuals I met, except where people have asked to use their real names or where their identities are a matter of public record.

I don't think it's necessary to worry too much about keeping track of who's who or what school people are from. To my great surprise, the students, and their allies, articulated a common message regardless of location. I think what is important is that we are hearing from students, teachers, and administrators on the frontlines and hearing the power of that unified voice. Hopefully, the distinctiveness and the verve and vigor of their voices will strike you as much as it did me and their individuality will accompany you throughout the book.

I provide a list of participants and their schools at the front of this book. But first, here is a very brief overview of the schools I visited, which are as diverse as the students themselves.

Burton School is a small school of approximately 150 students, Grades 11 and 12 only. Equity animates Burton School's climate.

Equity and social justice are the governing principles of Elizabeth Coyt Alternative School, a small school of under 500 students that teaches Grades 9 to 12.

Approximately 1,000 students attend nearby Sylvia Avenue Collegiate and Vocational School, which teaches Grades 9 to 12 and has a much more ethnically diverse student population than either Burton or Coyt.

Trimble Collegiate Institute is a hardscrabble high school of over 1,200 ethnically diverse students. However, I will always remember Trimble – and it may be your take-away as well – for its "student-identity walls." You will see what I mean.

Brookwood Collegiate and Vocational School is the largest school I visited. Much more rough-and-tumble than Trimble, its student body numbers almost 2,000, many of whom were described to me as "gangsters" and "rejects" – terms I heard at other schools as well. Even so, pockets of equity flourish in the vast wasteland here that ignores equity.

Grosvenor Secondary School was the only private school I visited. Its 400 students were dealing with its first gay-straight alliance went I met with students there, an issue that had caused some controversy in the student newspaper.

And finally, as Toronto's only high school program for LGBTQ students, Triangle was a revelation. By 2016, about 600 students had passed through its doors at Oasis Alternative Secondary School. Some of the most remarkable students in this book attend Triangle.

For teachers, guidance counsellors, social workers, principals, vice-principals, trustees, and others who read this book, I ask you as you meet the students and teachers and guidance counsellors from these wide-ranging schools to consider what goes on in *your* classroom, in *your* school? How do *you* conceptualize safety? Let this be your entry point.

I ask you, also, to consider that acceptance of homophobia is itself an act of homophobia. Complicity is tantamount to discrimination, and inaction in the face of hostility contributes to schools being unsafe for LGBTQ students. This is the final implicit message the people in this book are imparting to us.

No matter how long it may take, schools have to be transformed. Some change can be achieved immediately. Some change may take years. That is no reason not to start now. Don't believe me; believe them.

Acknowledgments

It is my great pleasure to thank the students and teachers who gave so generously of their time. This book would not have been possible without their commitment, courage, and candour. My thanks to Bruce Ryder, Didi Khayatt, Don Cochrane, Gerald Walton, Azmi Jubran, Gabe Picard, Ellen Chambers-Picard, the late Peter Corren, Murray Corren, Jeffrey White, Tim McCaskell, Stephen Myher, Adam Gingera, Steve Falkingham, and Randy Schmidt and all of the terrific people at UBC Press.

Finally, I acknowledge with gratitude the financial support provided by the Law Foundation of British Columbia and the Legal Research Institute at the University of Manitoba.

Participants

For some of the interviewees in this book, real names are used with their permission. Their work promoting equity and social justice in schools is a matter of public record. They are Murray Corren, Peter Corren, Azmi Jubran, Tim McCaskell, Gabe Picard, and Jeffrey White. I am grateful to each of them.

Except in the discussion of matters of public record, the names of the schools are fictitious, and the names of the students, teachers, and other allies are pseudonyms. There would be no book without any of these generous people.

The following list will help readers to keep track of the students and educators at each school. Of course, I met with and spoke with many more students and teachers than those who appear in this book. If I have not included them, it is mainly because their perspectives, stories, and ideas duplicated those who do appear. However, my thanks go to all who permitted me to spend time with them.

Burton School

Delores Kent – teacher
Lazy Daisy – Grade 12 student
Benjamin – Grade 12 student
Alexander – Grade 12 student
Brent – Grade 12 student

Sylvia Avenue Collegiate and Vocational School

Sharon Dominick – teacher
Melanie Bhatia – teacher
Barry – Grade 11 student
Louise – Grade 11 student
Douglas Allington – student who wrote a letter of thanks to
Sharon Dominick

Trimble Collegiate Institute

Lorna Gillespie – teacher who encouraged students to write
on the walls
Len – Grade 12 student
Katie – Grade 12 student

Elizabeth Coyt Alternative School

Carla – Grade 12 student, girlfriend of Emma
Emma – Grade 12 student, girlfriend of Carla
Cal – Grade 12 student, best friend of Emma and Carla

Brookwood Collegiate and Vocational School

Diana Goundrey – guidance counsellor
Joey – Grade 11 student who wrote poem
Sian – Grade 11 female student
Jerry – student who had graduated from Brookwood
two years before I met him
Dalton – Grade 12 student involved in LGBTQ politics
in Toronto
Kyle – Grade 12 student

Grosvenor Secondary School

Terrence – Grade 12 student
Sam – Grade 12 student
Mr. Taylor – teacher

Triangle Program at Oasis Alternative Secondary School

Ryan – Grade 9 student
James – Grade 10 student
Noel – Grade 12 student
Trista – Grade 11 transgender student
Silver – Grade 11 queer student
Jeffrey White – head of the Triangle Program

Others

Michael – Grade 12 student I met at an anti-bullying conference
Bruce – teacher I met at a conference in Toronto
Anders – high school principal, Vancouver
Alice – Grade 11 student, Vancouver

AM I SAFE HERE?

Introduction

At the beginning of the school year, we'd always run
through the school rules or whatever they were ...
But I would think to myself: I'm gay. Am I safe here?
— *Gabe Picard, Grade 12 student, Thunder Bay*

LGBTQ students are regularly excluded from full citizenship in their schools. Their outlaw status and "queer" citizenship put them at constant risk of exclusion, harassment, and bullying, thus forcing them to ask, as Gabe Picard does, "Am I safe here?"

Too often educators search for solutions to bullying at the level of the individual. This approach limits their ideas of bullying and victimization to the study of only a few implicated students rather than looking at the culture of the school.

Fortunately, research on bullying is now moving away from this narrow focus in order to consider how the culture of schools gives rise to bullying. Because school culture assumes that everybody is heterosexual, it validates heterosexuality. This bias conveys benefits and privileges to some students at the expense of those who do not fall into that category. And it is the students who transmit the values of the normative social order, often through bullying. Only by embracing this view of bullying as part of the larger school culture can solutions to bullying be realized.

This book is written for classroom teachers, administrators, school staff, trustees, staff developers, and pre-service teachers who want to promote student safety and school improvement by creating a safe and inclusive school for LGBTQ students. It asks that we stand back from the two or three students who might be involved in isolated instances of bullying, or even repeated bullying, and move instead toward a view that takes the cultural context of bullying into account.

Something Else Is Needed

Many of the students you will hear from in this book view negative attitudes and bias – in classrooms, extracurricular activities, cafeteria discussions, and hallway gossip – as more immediately threatening to their personal identities and safety than any fear of physical or verbal harassment or violence. In other words, there is a system of inequality, exclusion, and oppression that is organized around sexuality.[1] Everyone agrees that schools must ensure physical safety and have policies that respond to bullying as it occurs. But in the words of a principal I spoke with, "Something else is needed." This book tries to address that "something else."

Almost all of the students who speak with me talk about the pressures they face in simply walking the hallways. Len, a seventeen-year-old gay student in Grade 12, succinctly sums up that anxiety:

> In my early years, I avoided hallways because they were really ruled by this dominating self-validating culture in this school. The dominant culture was not violent, I wouldn't say, not violent or overly aggressive, or homophobic, but it was definitely very heterosexist. And [with] the cool kids hanging out and walking through that hallway, [it] was always a little bit uncomfortable for me.

For some students, however, the hallways are a clear threat to their physical safety. Gabe Picard describes what it is like simply going from one classroom to another:

All the hallways were terrifying to me. Always. I would always make sure that I was walking down the middle of the hallway. It's harder to actually body check me into the locker that way because when you're beside a locker, you're there, and it's convenient, so boom, they would just throw their weight into you.

Ryan, a fifteen-year-old student in the Triangle Program for LGBTQ students, left his previous school because of public persecution (somehow unseen by teachers?) that often occurred in the hallways:

It was really hard not only to be out, but you kind of got harassed in the hallways. Like, you'd have people yelling at you, and you just wanted to be left alone. I left because I really couldn't take it there anymore.

When I ask him whether he ever heard the word *fag* at his previous school, he says, "Oh yeah, in the halls, up and down." Did he have some way of dealing with it? "Yeah. I just didn't go to school."

These students negotiate the unsafe spaces of schools by making trade-offs, such as sticking to the middle of hallways, and by making impossible choices no student should have to make, such as just staying home. But they offer solutions, too. The students I meet, including Gabe Picard and Lazy Daisy, both in Grade 12, are part of a new student-led activism among LGBTQ youth who see the importance of a pro-found, embracing connectedness between LGBTQ students and their schools.

This book discusses some ways this connectedness can be accomplished. Several provinces, including Ontario, Manitoba, and Alberta, have introduced legislation that gives students the legal right to form gay-straight alliances.[2] This is a step in the right direction, but only a step. What we need to achieve in order to create a safe and welcoming space for LGBTQ students is recognition of queer realities and lives. Change in that direction has been under way in isolated places for years and is now becoming more commonplace and more sophisticated. For example, some students have already begun to argue that the term *gay-straight alliance* is bred from the very binary they wish to avoid. However, because legislation is framed in terms of gay-straight alliances, that is the term used in this book.

Even though more and more schools have anti-bullying or safe school policies, bullying is still familiar behaviour in schools. This is often because school policies and approaches are framed to respond only to physical, verbal, or even cyberbullying – and only after it has occurred. Responsive policies do little to change the culture that gives rise to bullying. I hope that as you read this book, you will come to see that physical bullying is only part of the problem faced by LGBTQ students. For us to fully appreciate why LGBTQ students feel unsafe in school, the entire cultural experience of going to school must be framed within this lens. Otherwise, looking at bullying but ignoring what is happening (or not happening) in the curriculum, in the schoolyards, and in the hallways and cafeterias is like looking at schools through a straw.

Students as Experts

One of the aims of this book is to listen to the stories of LGBTQ youth and their allies – the teachers and guidance counsellors who support them – in order to better appreciate their day-to-day experiences. So this book begins by asking students a simple question: "What is school like for you?"

My hope is that by presenting a sense of the realities of LGBTQ students in schools, in their own voices, this book will create a picture of the social setting that gives rise to the bullying, harassment, and exclusion they experience.

In 2002, Gabe Picard, a gay Grade 12 student in Thunder Bay, brought a human rights complaint against the Lakehead District School Board, claiming discrimination based on sexual orientation. His complaint argued that because he was being bullied and because the school board had failed to provide a safe and inclusive school environment, he was being denied access to the education that was available to everybody else. Here was a student heroically taking on the cultural brickwork of schools, not just concerned about his own personal safety. Gabe tells me about his decision to file a complaint:

> I got really, really fed up and I went into the principal's office, and I yelled at her and I told her, "Well, you're still letting this happen." And she's like, "Well, what do you want me to do about it, Gabe? We can't change the way it is." She told me that. Those were her exact words: "Gabe, we can't change the culture."
>
> That's what set me off, and then I told her that, if she couldn't change the culture, then she'd failed as an educator and that she was a failure as an educator.
>
> And I said, "What's the point in you becoming an educator, then, if you can't change the culture? That's the whole thing."
>
> That's what I told her. I told her, "*That's the whole thing*, that's what teaching is all about. Change." And then I told her that she failed as an educator if she believed she couldn't change it, and then I stormed out. So that's why I did it, filed the human rights complaint.

I ask you to consider Gabe Picard as you read every page of this book because I believe that LBGTQ students are the experts on their own experiences and lives and can best address the fundamental aims of this book.

This book is part of the shift in focus from seeing bullying primarily as a psychological problem to questioning the sociocultural processes of normalization and the structures of power that hold them in place. As the students in this book talk about their lives, they question the formal and informal laws and codes that govern high schools and regulate student behaviours.

The need to transform the culture of schools emerged as a consistent theme in my conversations with students and teachers. Several years after Gabe Picard brought his action, Katie, a Grade 12 student, tells me that "transforming the culture is what it's all about. *It's the fucking map, the compass, and the moon, all in one*. It's everything queers need to find our way out of oppression and the only thing that will do it."

Some schools are doing terrific work to include LGBTQ students, but they are oases among the vast wasteland of schools that continue to forget, oppress, and exclude these students. In some schools, the students themselves are leading the way. But in every school, this work needs to be the work of every teacher, every administrator, every staff member, every trustee, and every citizen.

By the time you reach the end of this book, you may find the term *bullying* to be mostly inadequate to describe the social predicament of LGBTQ students. Because, for many, it is much more than that. What LGBTQ students live in fear of encountering and do encounter is the day-to-day exclusion and oppression that goes on in every school. In 2013, I attended a cultural festival in Vancouver while interviewing teachers for this book. I spoke with Anders, the principal of a local high school, who addressed the difference between bullying and the larger cultural position of LGBTQ students very effectively:

> I think *bullying* is a less challenging word for teachers and administrators than having to confront something larger like heterosexism and homo-phobia ... You only have to worry about a few people rather than using a wider lens to assess a bigger picture of what's going on. Bullying – it's simpler and makes for a simpler target ... Something else is needed, but where do you start?

Based on the interviews and observations in this book, it seems that what is needed for LGBTQ students is to be connected with and included in their school culture. This book envisions a future where the unequal treatment of LGBTQ students cannot even be imagined.

One School, Many Laws

Mindful of Gabe's and Katie's words about transforming the culture, I have spoken with students, teachers, and others about the spaces, rules, and norms in the lives of LGBTQ students, which together comprise the space that the students in this book would describe as "my school." But every school is made up of smaller, varied spaces: classrooms, hallways, playgrounds, the cafeteria, locker rooms, and so on. Norms and rules, both formal and informal, govern those spaces, dictate behaviours, and assign positions. As state agents, teachers and administrators have a duty to ensure the safety and equality of LGBTQ students in all schools, as well as their freedom from discrimination in all aspects of school life and culture, including the school curriculum. But how to do that?

Cultural norms interact with formal law and official policies in schools and can carry as much authority as law. For many students, these norms, law-like in their own right, may have an even more powerful influence on student behaviours and attitudes. The formal policy of the state may say one thing, but what do students' peers say? Their family? Their religious beliefs? Their ingrained sense of gender? Can we assume that even well-written laws and policies dealing with harassment, bullying, or inclusiveness will have their intended effects? What is the influence of cultural expectations on the effectiveness of law and policies? On student behaviours and attitudes? On the climate of schools? In what ways do students monitor each other and model themselves on the values within our normative social order?

This book emphasizes LGBTQ students' everyday experiences to show the effects of these official and unofficial standards. I take this approach because it's needed to understand why formal law often struggles to deal with the harassment and bullying of these students.

I hope that the voices presented here comprise new knowledge about what must be changed to create safe, equitable, and inclusive schools for LGBTQ students. Throughout, students speak in support of nothing less than changing their entire cultural experience of going to school. The students and teachers who tell their stories here make a number of suggestions for improving school culture and creating an equitable, inclusive environment. Their suggestions are summarized at the end of each chapter.

If you are a teacher, an administrator, or a staff member, ask yourself how much of what you hear from the students in this book applies to your own school. Listen, and we can learn what must be done.

1

Changing the Culture

This is what the culture does. It threatens us in so
many ways.

> – *Lazy Daisy, Grade 12 student, Toronto*

Historically, LGBTQ youth have felt excluded and ignored by most
Canadian institutions – even their families – leaving them hurt, alienated,
or dead from suicide or from violence perpetrated against them.[1] Now
that the problem of bullying in schools has been identified and confirmed,[2] the work of applying that knowledge must begin to make schools
more inclusive and equitable for LGBTQ students.

I found LGBTQ students to be keenly aware – more so than the average student – of their own school's safe school policies and articulate
about what is needed to improve, if not change, the culture of schools
for themselves and other LGBTQ youth. So, rather than focusing on hard
statistics or pie charts, I present, in their own words, how these students
define and understand *bullying* and *safety*. I asked them to tell me how
their schools actually pursue safety and to think about how to translate
this knowledge into new laws. As Alice, a Grade 11 student from Vancouver,
puts it,

> At my school, they talk about safety and this Erase Bullying program they
> just started, but that just means security and punishment or even just a

lot of talk, at least so far. Dos and don'ts. There's a contaminated environment at my school for queer kids that has nothing to do with that kind
of safety.

Not surprisingly, most of the students feel that *safety* has to be defined
broadly in order to have a significant impact on the school culture, not
defined just in terms of responses undertaken following incidents of
bullying and harassment.

Heteronormativity Isn't Safety

What surprised me most was the extent to which LGBTQ students used
the word *equity* when talking about safety. For them, *safe schools* means
creating schools that are equitable. They acknowledge that safety means
ensuring physical safety for all students. And they all believe that safety
means keeping weapons out of school and responding to physical violence
when it occurs. But they also agree that this kind of approach alone is
not enough.

What is more important to students is addressing the heteronormativity of their schools – especially the curriculum. Many view heteronormativity as more immediately threatening to their personal identities
and safety than bullying or than any fear of physical or verbal harassment
or violence. They acknowledge, however, that students in many schools
– even in other major city schools but especially in smaller cities and in
rural settings – do have significant concerns about physical and verbal
violence.

Many schools confront the problem of bullying by focusing on security, equating *safe schools* with surveillance cameras, security guards,
dress codes, and mandatory ID badges for students and teachers. For most
students, the safe school policies are not concerned with equity. This
oversight is a telling gap. When schools officially recognize and embrace
LGBTQ inclusiveness, heterosexual students will do so as well.

However, for a very few schools I visited, safety *is* framed as an issue
of equity and inclusiveness. But what *is* an equitable framework? What
does that mean? And what do equity and inclusiveness look like? The

Am I Safe Here?

theatre has a maxim: "Show, don't tell." And so, on cue, here are the students and teachers to speak for themselves. Lights up!

A Safe School Is an Equitable School Is an Inclusive School

"It's here somewhere," Lazy Daisy says. I have been at Lazy Daisy's school, Burton, for a few weeks, and I have spent a good deal of time with her – lunch, a spare, and now an art class. I am in no rush to say goodbye. Earlier in the day, we completed a more formal interview-conversation that lasted about ninety minutes. Lazy Daisy does not like being referred to as a "woman." "I'm a girl. I'm not a woman and I'm not a lesbian." She describes herself as "pansexual," typical of the varied vocabulary many LGBTQ students in schools use to describe their sexual and gender identities and typical of the awareness most possess of the power of words and definitions. Lazy Daisy does sometimes refer to herself as "gay," a term I have noticed female students using more frequently than I would have expected.

After our formal interview that morning, Lazy Daisy showed me a print she had made that, in her view, more accurately addresses the kind of oppression that queer kids face in school, which, in her words, is not "just about bullying." When I asked her whether I could make a photocopy of the print, she offered to make me an original and asked me to meet her in her art class later that day. And here we are.

The art teacher is nowhere to be seen, but Lazy Daisy assures me this is not unusual. "This school is cool," she tells me, still rummaging through an overstuffed backpack. Finally, she finds the crumpled sheet she's been looking for and hands it to me. "Here it is," she says. As I look it over, she says, "It's a piece of crap."

I read the caption out loud: "Be confident. Bullies don't like people who are not afraid." "Elmer the Safety Elephant," I say. "It looks like it's a hundred years old." She reaches for the sheet and takes it from me as though she hasn't seen it before, shakes her head, and tells me the story behind it. "I got this from my friend Jane. This is the kind of shit they're handing out at her school. It was in a booklet or something, so I tore it out." Her anger, she tells me, has two bases. First, she is angry that the message of the image is that the burden of being bullied is on students.

Second, she feels that the image is infantile and misses out on the complexity of what "really goes on when somebody is being bullied, especially if they're queer, for God's sake."

As Lazy Daisy and I talk, she moves around the back of the art class, opening jars and mixing paints and carrying on conversations with the other students, who show little curiosity about me and what I am doing. Now she is at some sort of printmaking machine that I do not recognize from any art class I ever took, and I mention this. "LD" – as she asks me to call her – assures me that the equipment at her school is superior to that found at most high schools in the district. I do not ask her how she knows this, but it is obvious that she and other students I meet at Burton School regard their school as "special" and "not like other schools."

As Lazy Daisy prepares to create a print, I ask her a question I ask everyone: Is she aware of any policies or laws that are in place in Ontario or in her school dealing with safety? Lazy Daisy explains that her school emphasizes "equity as safety." Every other student at Burton confirms that this school pursues "safety" in terms of doing "equity." Lazy Daisy tells me,

> There's no doubt about it that ... equity ... is going to do a hell of a lot more for the safety of queer kids ... At this school, the school uses the equity stuff to create a safe school environment. But I don't think you could get that going at every school. Everybody's too afraid of the gangsters and rejects at other schools. You could get some pockets of that happening if teachers or guidance would support it, but otherwise queer kids are pretty much on their own unless they're at a school like this, and there aren't a lot like this.

Lazy Daisy makes two prints, both wet when she hands them to me. "You can't go yet," she says. "I can talk while they dry."

I ask Lazy Daisy to explain to me exactly how "equity" can possibly be equated with "safety." She thinks for a beat, checks the condition of her prints, and then tells me, "Safety for queer kids is about changing things, not protecting things. I mean, of course, you have to protect kids, but that's a given, isn't it? But it's not just about bullying, I mean, in a physical way. We're bullied by just the culture we're in."

Am I Safe Here?

She tells me that the idea for her "anti-Elmer" art "occurred to [her] in gay and lesbian studies class." I am a bit taken aback that her curriculum includes gay and lesbian content. She is taken aback by my surprise:

> Oh, yeah. I was in gay and lesbian studies, and I was just looking at the statistics of drug use and suicide among gay people as opposed to straight teens. And the results were actually, like, appalling, because it's amazing how much more at risk I think queer teens are. Three times more at risk [of] suicide than straight teens growing up in high school because they have to face so much more in terms of the culture. So I made this really cool print that shows all that. It's anti-Elmer.

When I ask her to explain in greater detail what the print represents, she continues:

> It's a mirror, it's what you see when you're queer and you look in the mirror. It's the question we ask every day. And it has lines on it. And the lines are the rainbow flag. See, these are the colours. And it's got a little razor, and it's got "Am i @ RISK?" And there's a needle going into it, into the "A." And like the "R" is a joint. This is what the culture does, it threatens us in so many ways.

"Am i @ RISK?" by Lazy Daisy, Burton School

As I watch Lazy Daisy make her print for me, she moves with ease around the art class, yelling out to her classmates – and the teacher, who has returned – that she is making another "Am i @ RISK?" print "for Donn – have you met Donn? Unless you're queer, he doesn't want to talk to you. We're talking revolution back here."

Lazy Daisy and many of the students I meet represent a trend in schools: students making a difference by contributing to a school culture. I ask Lazy Daisy about the question mark at the end of her "Am i @ RISK?" artwork. She waits before answering but eventually admits that she is tired of the negative portrayals of queer youth as suicidal and troubled – as true as this predicament is for many and borne out by statistics:

> So I wanted to do this project and show that, if there's problems, it's systemic. So I want people to think about *why*. So I put that in. And I think a lot of it has to do with religious belief and culture. I have mixed views on this because it's not just what colour you are but, like, how you're raised and the parents you have. I'm done with the extreme negative consequences like in my old school. It's like a cue on negative. I love my school, this school, and I love what we're all doing. And I don't know, I just wanted to do a positive reaction to that fact.

Student-Led Activism

Students like Gabe Picard and Lazy Daisy are part of a new student-led activism among LGBTQ youth who see how important it is for LGBTQ students to have a consistent, embracing connection with their schools. That kind of connectedness must include all students. Gabe puts it this way:

> I've been interviewed by other people before, and they always want me to go through the incidents, what happened. But I can't. I can't ever actually pull it out like that. You know, "this happened, and this and this happened, and everything got worse and worse." I feel like when I talk about it, it seems like it's *less* to people than it actually was. That's what

I always think. I think that it's sounding like less than it actually was because nobody tried to ... beat me up every day, but I'm trying to get across that it was *big*. The way it *is*. What people *say*. How they *are*. Because it was all the time – it was just there. It was the entire culture. People don't get that. It wasn't safe.

He tells me how inadequate it is to view threats to queer students solely as individual incidents of bullying, even escalating incidents. His depiction of the harassment as "big" seems insightful to me, a powerful condemnation of policy intervention based solely on a law and order response. I ask Gabe to tell me how equity and inclusiveness are pursued at his school. He laughs.

You're kidding. At one point, they bought some door hangers to go on the doorknobs – the school did – and it said "Safe Space" on it, but they didn't even *know* what that meant.

They even brought those to the mediation for the case, and they're like, "Oh we bought some rainbow flags for the doorknobs." And then of course, being super prepared, like, we were, with our bajillions of bags, I'm like, and I pull one out, I'm like, "These ones?"

They're like, "Yeah, those are the ones, yeah." And I'm like, "But what does that mean?" I looked right at them and asked, "But what does that mean – 'Safe Space'?"

And they didn't even know what it meant. They didn't even know what it meant. They had nothing to say. Safe schools, safe space, they had nothing to say. Because it's so big, what makes school safe for us, and they didn't get it.

LGBTQ students are not content to be labelled "at risk." They are speaking up and demanding a presence in the culture of the school around them – one that is not just tolerated (yesterday's approach) but instead welcomed and celebrated. Gabe wants to change the culture; Lazy Daisy and other students I meet want to be acknowledged but also embraced by the culture. Daisy does not want to talk very much about making sure that schools are merely free of negative influences as a way to provide a safe, equitable, and inclusive education for students like her. "That's a given." For Daisy, the solution lies in overcoming the obstacles to welcoming and embracing queer students:

> Safe, nurturing, positive, and respectful can go out the window when all of a sudden you're talking about queers ... We're the ones experiencing the violence in such different ways. And if queers do drugs, it's to escape what's happening to them. I like my statement better.

I tell her about Gabe, one of the few people I have spent time with whose experiences and statements are a matter of public record. She says,

> That's exactly it. You've got to change a culture. You've got to do more than take away – what was it? – negative factors. You've got to put in some positive factors. That's why for my school, it's more about equity.
>
> About that Thunder Bay guy [Gabe], he's right. If you just punish people for homophobic attitudes and stuff like that, or incidents of outright homophobia, like when there's discrimination and people attacking other people, it's not gonna help. Even with crime in general, I think it's about changing the attitude, the root of the problem, not just doing something about an isolated incident. That guy is right.

Can You Change the Culture?

As a researcher, however, my question is about the extent to which any policy or declaration of inclusiveness can have so broad a reach. "Is it possible," I ask Lazy Daisy, "to change an entire culture? How do you do that?" She is quick to identify what I believe is the key factor in changing the climate of schools for LGBTQ students:

> Well you start young, right? By implementing programs in school like anti-racism programs. There's Black History Month, there's all sort of things like that, but there's nothing for gay people. I mean, at my old school, they just started a Pride event, but it was a joke. They were just making the teachers do it. I feel there's not a lot of focus on it.

Daisy goes to find something in which to store my print. "Yeah," she says. "Nurturing and positive. That's what we do here. For the most part ... We *contribute*, you know?" She talks about how Burton School differs from other schools in the neighbourhood:

> [Elizabeth Coyt Alternative School] has a much larger population than us and a different kind of environment, and they have a bigger budget than we do, basically. But we have our own things. We don't have the large events they do, but we have our own things. [Burton School] is the best school I've ever been to. It's very accepting. Even with gay guys like Alexander and Benjamin, the straight guys will joke around with them. We even have an out teacher who has a partner.

She explains that Burton School's gay and lesbian studies course has contributed to this culture of equity and inclusivity: "I think courses like this make that possible. It just sends a message, you know. Oh, I just love my school."

Lazy Daisy and I are almost finished our time together. "Your print is still wet," she tells me. "So you can't put it in this envelope yet. Actually, I made you two in case you fuck one of them up." I thank Daisy for the print, and the spare, and point out that artists usually sign their work. "But you can't use your real name," I add. She brightens. "Can I choose my own phony name?" She writes "Lazy Daisy" on both prints. "And can you call me that?" I assure her that she is in charge of naming her identity on all counts. "Elmer the Safety Elephant is whack," the artist now known as Lazy Daisy announces. She laughs and is already talking with another student as she leaves the room.

Summing Up

School culture needs to be inclusive of LGBTQ students, recognizing, reflecting, and celebrating their lives. Incident-based policies, which target participants, are insufficient. Laws and policies must do more than just punish bullies. Safety must mean more than surveillance cameras, security guards, dress codes, and mandatory ID tags for students and teachers.

Schools must acknowledge the presence of LGBTQ students but must do more than simply underscore the differences between LGBTQ students and others. LGBTQ students deserve to have their experiences affirmed. Without these approaches, surveillance cameras, security guards, and dress codes do nothing to make schools safe for LGBTQ students. In fact, for many of these students, many schools, as they are presently configured, are spaces that do harm.

What Needs to Be Done

- Students must talk about the need for a culture change or a change in school climate rather than focusing only on bullying. New policies must then incorporate students' ideas.
- School administrators, teachers, and staff must recognize that what is needed is a culture change, not a policy to deal with bullying after it has occurred.
- Schools must embrace and include LGBTQ lives and queer realities in official spaces.
- The work of changing the culture of the school needs to start as early as kindergarten and continue through Grade 12.

The next chapters develop and expand on these ideas and illustrate that this kind of work does not have to be limited to social studies classes but can be a part of all classrooms in all subject areas.

Am I Safe Here?

2

How Safe Is My School?

I can't help noticing your walls. Are most of the classrooms like this?

– Donn Short

According to the students I meet, schools pursue safety in a range of different ways, corresponding to the degree to which the safety concerns and needs of LGBTQ students are considered. The conceptualizations of safety could be represented on a spectrum like this:

Control   Security   Equity   Social justice

At one end of the spectrum are schools where safety is conceptualized, discussed, and interpreted as an extreme in which *control* of the identity of the students is paramount. In this arrangement, the students are read as dangerous – particularly black male students. Safety measures are perceived by students and their allies as trying to "whiten" student identities. Dress codes that restrict clothing often associated with hip hop, such as baggy pants and hats, are especially emphasized by school safety committees.

At other schools, *security* is still the primary focus but with less emphasis on controlling nonwhite student identities. Measures include surveillance cameras, security guards, and mandatory student and teacher ID tags.

In schools at the *control-security* end of the spectrum, equity policies are secondary to concerns about violence and the presence of gangs in the school. Schools in these categories perceive their own students as the threat to having a safe school. Most schools fall into these two categories.

Further along the spectrum are schools that promote *equity* as a means of achieving a safe and secure environment for students, teachers, and staff. These schools do not focus on monitoring their own students. In fact, they empower their students.

At the other extreme on the safety spectrum are schools that not only promote equity but also actively pursue goals of *social justice*. The chief ingredient of this classification is a proactive approach in which equity is looked for in the school environment and sought in the larger community as well. Students at these schools are encouraged and taught to consider how race, class, gender, and sexuality intersect and are sites of multiple oppression.

The students and teachers you are about to hear from are the ones who created these classifications. I believe their observations, stories, and words confirm the truth of looking at schools through this lens.

Safety as Control: Sylvia Avenue Collegiate and Vocational School

At the end of my first day at Sylvia Avenue Collegiate and Vocational School, teacher Sharon Dominick walks me to the front door. "This is certainly out of your way, Sharon. You really don't have to do that." Sharon assures me that she wants to make sure I know the way out of the school and do not get lost: "I don't want the students to think you don't know where you're going. I just want to make sure you get on your way okay." I thank her, tell her I will see her again tomorrow, and walk out of the front entrance of Sylvia Avenue. I walk slowly around the building to take some photographs – I take photos at every school I visit.

I prefer to take pictures when students are not around, but sometimes this is not possible. I take a few shots and head down the tree-lined street that is a direct route to the subway. Thirty yards out the front door of the school, I walk by a group of male students I have not noticed, but who, evidently, have noticed me. One of them yells out, "Hey, white boy, you a fag?"

Security Guards, Surveillance Cameras, and ID Tags
Earlier in the day, I met Sharon in the classroom where she teaches media and English. In today's lesson, Sharon introduces her English class to the concept of a white-nonwhite binary opposition of race. She has divided the class into two groups, one composed of white students and the other of nonwhite students. She asks them to consider a list of questions on the book they have just read, Harper Lee's *To Kill a Mockingbird* (1960), and on broader themes of race. Later, they will come together as one group and compare answers. For now, she wants them to feel they are two distinct groups, one white and the other nonwhite. As they are working loudly on the assignment, several arguments break out. Sharon returns to the side of the class where I am watching and sits next to me. "What are those tags they're all wearing?" I ask her.

"Lanyards. ID tags. A lot of the students miss classes because of those lanyards. If they forget to wear them or don't have them with them, they're not allowed in the building."

"Even if you know who they are and they're in your class?" I ask her.

"That's right. You should talk with Melanie, one of the teachers here. She's even more opinionated than I am about the lanyards."

"I can't help noticing your walls. Are most of the classrooms like this?" The walls of Sharon's classroom are almost entirely covered in images from the media – most of which address some form of sexism, homophobia, racism, or class oppression. Sharon uses these images to get her students to think about the interconnected issues of oppression. She calls this "culture jamming."

"Check out the rest of the school," Sharon advises me wryly.

Sharon tells me about a former student of hers named Jason. Two years ago, one of Sharon's students called Jason a "fucking faggot" in class. The student who shouted these words at him was a Muslim girl. In

Sharon's words, Jason "stood up to her" and called her a "bitch." Sharon tells me, "So obviously, he wanted her to feel the sting of words. And what was the response of the administration here? They encouraged Jason to switch schools. They were both suspended, and basically, the administration forced him to go to another school eventually." Sharon is angry telling me the story, even though it occurred some time ago. She wrote a letter of protest to the administration. As Sharon explains to me, "That girl's statement was unmotivated hate speech. What Jason said, he said defending himself. You don't have the same expectations when people react because they are being attacked."

The administration responded by instituting a gay-straight alliance (GSA) – but for teachers only. I'm sure I've misheard. "For teachers? Only?" Sharon nods.

> It was for teacher training, but it was painful and I couldn't take it for very long. I think it was a liability thing or they wouldn't have done it. The attitude was: "We're providing training, what more can we do?" Teachers went to it, but nobody cared. Nobody wanted to be there. I heard homophobic comments the entire time I was there. One of the teachers there said about Jason, "I don't have any problems with those kinds of people, but what does he expect when he's flaunting it?" Mercifully, the whole group died.

Following the demise of the teacher-only GSA, Sharon and Melanie Bhatia, a teacher I will soon meet, decided to start a Student League for Social Justice. Sharon explains, "That's the sort of thing they do at Burton School or Coyt all the time, and I thought we should do it here, where it could really do some good. But it didn't last long. The administration didn't like it."

Looking around at the photos, music lyrics, and images on her wall, I say to her: "Well, your classroom is the kind of room the students will remember years from now." Sharon smiles at this, thinking for a moment. "At this school, safety is framed as an issue of control, not equity. Security guards, surveillance cameras, always talking about crime and the dress code. There's a toxic environment at this school. It's not safe for students." I ask her what this school is like for LGBTQ students. Sharon's answer is immediate:

Am I Safe Here?

It's not a safe school because teachers don't challenge homophobia. The whole "it's so gay" thing. The use of the word *fag* by students – by teachers! I tell the students that using those words threatens the security of gay kids, makes them and me feel threatened. They don't get it because that's not part of the message of what it means to be secure or safe around here.

What Sharon is talking about, of course, is one of the results of schools framing safety in terms of seeing their own and not the larger culture. Recall that Gabe Picard told me that he filed his human rights action because he wanted to change the culture. But many policies opt instead to focus on safety and bullying as generic concepts, removed from culture. Generic policies are often justified as creating safety "for everybody," not just for "one specific group." But this approach lacks any specific mention of the individual needs of LGBTQ students. And so there are two security guards at Sylvia Avenue and only sporadic pockets of equity created by the teachers and students who insist upon it in individual classrooms.

A Matter of Respect
When I meet Melanie later in the week, she tells me that she thinks the security guards are abusive to the students. Melanie is originally from "the Islands." Entering teaching in 1981, she taught "Native kids" for less than a year before returning to school to study theology. When Melanie first came to Sylvia Avenue, she regarded the school as a "safety net," a "safe place" for visible-minority students and students from low-income families who had been tossed out by other schools. No longer holding this view of her school, Melanie now views Sylvia Avenue, and other schools with significant visible-minority populations, as places that are decidedly unsafe. Melanie has strong opinions about how safety is pursued at this school. I do not have to ask many questions, but I do ask her how safety is put into effect in the school's daily practices. She says,

> In my opinion, with the dress code, lanyard, security guards, and surveillance cameras, the school is a prison. If this makes schools safe, then why isn't it implemented in all the schools? ... But it is not. These rules only

operate in certain schools, our school, with large minority populations. The message is clear. These schools have dangerous kids.

This message is articulated all around the school, even as you enter the building. An enormous stone sign on the garbage-strewn lawn at the main entrance announces the name of the school, which is difficult to read because of all the graffiti. In the guidance office and in the main office, where students wait to meet with the administration, there are piles of pamphlets quite different from what I saw at Burton School or what I will subsequently find at Elizabeth Coyt Alternative School. At those two schools, posters and handouts are geared toward university, study abroad, issues of equity, and even social justice – like Lazy Daisy's self-made "Queer Safety" art. Sylvia Avenue offers students pamphlets explaining the Youth Criminal Justice Act and warning students of the consequences of being charged as an adult.

Melanie and I talk for a long time about what she describes as "the socially constructed dangers at Sylvia Avenue." She speaks of the "self-fulfilling prophecies" associated with the treatment particularly of black male students. Regarded as innately dangerous and low-achieving, "even though they are not," these students "internalize this school's treatment until they break." For Melanie, the members of her school's Safe School Committee "formulate and implement safety protocols" that "create a narrative that practically guarantees that result." Melanie explains how she views the trajectory of these students within her school and its treatment of them:

> These kids are always being targeted from the minute they enter the school, and then they have to look for new families. This is the way they decide to get their power, through gangs or guns. If they cannot get [acceptance] and feel empowered in the school itself, then they just give up and they go for anything that represents power to them.
>
> And unfortunately, today, it's violence and gangs and guns. And I really feel that our school has contributed in turning a lot of our students, black males, into violent young men.

I ask Melanie whether Sylvia Avenue is a violent school and whether there have been any recent incidents of violence here. The question seems to pain her. After a moment, she takes a deep breath and explains,

> The truth is it's ongoing. A lot of things cause the kids to lose their temper. If they're just walking along the hallway, the security guard might just stop and say, "Show me your lanyard. Where's your ID?" And the fact that the kids have to take it out to show it or put it around their neck, and even the tone of voice that the guards use to ask them to produce their ID, I think a lot of the kids feel disrespected, and some of them lose their temper and ... so, it's ongoing. And then, of course, the school responds to these incidents by removing the student rather than examining its own role in creating this incident or, in fact, the general climate of unsafety when the school is supposed to be doing just the opposite and making the school a safe place.

Sharon offers her view on her school's refusal to conceptualize safety in terms of doing equity:

> There's an intelligence and creative freedom at other schools, but here it's a police mentality focusing on getting rid of the so-called dangerous students. Academically, the focus is on content, but I treat them all like they're going to university.
>
> As teachers, we should come to the table prepared for equity. If the students here go into Burton School or Coyt, they're suspended.
>
> The students in Burton School and Coyt are scared of our students. They don't come here.

The Threat from Within?

It is clear that Sharon Dominick conducts herself and her classroom in opposition to the general pattern of enforcement around her. Sharon is viewed by the students as a person of some leadership in the school – because she is white. Sharon and Melanie, however, believe the real power in the school is held by the male physical-education and tech-department teachers. As members of Sylvia Avenue's Safe School Committee and Dress Code Committee, they are pointed to as the voices who dictate how safety is pursued at the school.

In Melanie's opinion, the power of rules is used to control students, not to make school space safer. Of course, for Melanie, safety means equity and inclusiveness. Melanie explains to me that the power wielded by her school's Safe School and Dress Code Committees lies in their ability to suspend and expel students:

> Now, this is a very heavy thing, to get rid of students, but they do it under this whole umbrella of making the school safe for students. And that's how it started, this acquisition of power.
>
> Each school is able to have a Safe School Committee and a Dress Code Committee. Yes, because the board allows them to have these suspension and expulsion policies. These are very powerful groups because they really do make the rules. Nobody really wants to go against their rules. Once the committee votes on these regulations, it passes. I call them the "power committees."

Melanie understands who occupies leadership positions in the school and who does not. She offers a calm assessment of her own role in the school. She describes herself as "a colonized person." She is well aware of the difference that race makes when students seek help, particularly minority students:

> I know for myself, the students see that I am one of the unimportant visible-minority teachers in the school. They know that if they need help, they have to look to the white teachers who are either in the tech department or who are closer to the administration. And that's the only way they can get help.
>
> I, as a visible-minority teacher, know this as well. So when my students come for help, I have to look around for a white teacher to tell them the problem the student has in order for them to get help. So the kids know that there's a difference of power. And when you're white, you're empowered; when you are of colour, you have no power.

Until two years ago, Sylvia Avenue had a white principal. The current principal is a black man. I ask whether this makes any difference in the school. Melanie tells me that when the new principal arrived, he "opened up" the "power committees" to other teachers. Melanie volunteered to contribute to both the Safe School Committee and the Dress Code Committee. She joined both but felt her input was ignored. Melanie recognized that the two "power committees" were trying to "shape the identity of our students."

In Melanie's opinion, the rules are aimed solely at black students. As she puts it, "most of what the school was concerned with was controlling who they were. One of the first things the school did was to implement a 'hat policy.'"

Why a hat policy? "Students were not allowed to cover their heads – no hats or head coverings of any kind," Melanie says. Sharon, Melanie, and the students I speak with understand the rule to be directed at keeping students' faces visible for the benefit of the two security guards who patrol the school's corridors and cafeteria, as well as for the surveillance cameras.

For Melanie, the committees reconstituted the school in two ways. First, given the way the rules were written and enforced, black students were eliminated from the school's population. Second, the rules reconstructed the students who stayed in the school as "white." The official rules of the school were used to reinforce dominant social relations and to restrict the cultural identities produced in the school. This can be seen as the social construction of whiteness through law and policy.

LGBTQ: Not Part of the Agenda

The effect of this approach to safety on students of colour is worthy of its own study, but what is the significance of this approach for LGBTQ students? Targeting visible-minority students has a corresponding and inevitable chilling effect on the environment of the school for LGBTQ students.

First, LGBTQ students remain ignored. At Sylvia Avenue and other schools that pursue this construction of safety, LGBTQ youth are ignored or incidentally considered when administrations are compelled to do so.

Schools like Sylvia Avenue tend to regard the threat to student safety as coming from the general student population, not from any cultural licence to bully. Not only are LGBTQ students ignored when schools adopt a generic "hunker down" mentality that sees safety in terms of control and security, but that kind of climate also gives rise to an implied permission to threaten LGBTQ students.

LGBTQ students are threatened by homophobic or transphobic language that goes unchecked and is sometimes even encouraged – as we will see. When LGBTQ students hear words such as *fag* or *queer*, or worse, the safety of these students is threatened. If students, and sometimes teachers, feel an unchallenged permission to use these words, LGBTQ students wonder what other permissions have been given that threaten their safety.

It is not necessary that this kind of language be directed at LGBTQ students. The casual use of "that's so gay" as a disapproving remark raises questions of how welcome and safe LGBTQ students are. Just hearing its permissible use threatens LGBTQ students. This language can be heard on a daily basis in schools, many times a day, in the schoolyard, locker rooms, cafeteria, hallways, and often in the classroom itself. LGBTQ students hear these words and are pushed from the "normal" centre as the school defines it.

Both Sharon and Melanie tell me that LGBTQ students will never "come out" at Sylvia Avenue. "Sexual-minority students are not on the administration's radar, and they know it," Melanie tells me.

> I am aware of one girl that tried to come out. I think when they do want to come out, they get bullied and picked on. They transfer to Coyt as soon as they are in Grade II. So as far as I'm concerned, kids would be afraid to come out here if they're gay and lesbian because nobody respects anybody here. It's a whole cycle of control of some, neglect of others.

What Melanie and Sharon object to is the general climate of "safety as control," which actually leads to the very problems the Safe School Committee intended to target and eliminate. In particular, Sharon and Melanie underscore the summary way that students, who are the targeted victims of this control, rebel against it and then are removed from the school for doing so. They complain about the complete refusal of the school to conceptualize safety in terms of doing equity, an approach they believe is the only way to create safe schools for LGBTQ students as well as for visible minority students and others.

Melanie concludes, "So I think the whole idea of safety and controlling who the students are, they sort of blurred that whole thing. And gay kids, not part of that agenda."

What Students Say about It

I find no "out" students at Sylvia Avenue. Two of Sharon's students, Barry and Louise, both in Grade 11, are introduced to me as "questioning." Although they have agreed to talk with me, they are not very forthcoming, even in a confidential interview. Both Louise and Barry admit to being verbally abused by homosexual epithets, but only Barry acknowledges being gay. He has written a personal piece for English class identifying his "ideal partner" as a boy. Louise denies that she is questioning.

Both Barry and Louise have identified safety as an issue of doing equity in Sharon Dominick's English class. But according to them, the administration does not view safety that way. "Just lanyards," Barry responds with a grin. "They talk a lot about lanyards."

Sharon tells me that Barry is one of her favourite students. She smiles every time Barry is in her classroom. He is a small, always smiling, fifteen-year-old Asian boy. Only when he moves across the classroom do you have any sense of the television character on whom Barry has obviously patterned his physical gestures: Jack McFarland of the sitcom *Will & Grace* (1998–2006). Sharon has tipped me off in advance.

Barry talks quietly about being verbally abused at his school. He cannot bring himself to use words like *fag* or *queer,* so I write the words down on a piece of paper, and he looks at me and nods, "Yes, those were the words. Especially that one," he says, pointing to "fag."

Barry tells me that Sylvia Avenue is "a school of rejects. It's where everybody goes when they don't really know where to go or don't really like the other schools."

"Why do you come here?" I ask him. "Do you have a choice?"

"Yes. I could go to another school, but my friends are here. I come here to be with my friends."

I ask whether this is a safe school for LGBTQ students. "No. Gay students are kind of ignored. They don't have the cameras for gay students." I can see Barry is thinking about his answer. Then he adds, "Well, the administration ignores gay students, [but] the students don't. You feel like you've got to stay in line. If you don't, well, who can you count on to look after you then? You only really feel safe in Miss Dominick's class. It's a different world in there."

When Barry and I finish talking and he walks away, he resumes his Jack McFarland imitation. This is how he copes.

Every Teacher? Not without Institutional Support

Both Melanie and Sharon believe that inclusive education is the best means by which the larger cultural licence to condemn LGBTQ students can be refuted. Melanie explains,

> The curriculum leaders did not think equity was an important enough issue on which to have a committee. And I called them on it because I said, "You have a paper committee in the school that deals with what to do with paper, but you don't have equity?" And many schools in Toronto do look at equity as an important issue. Look at Coyt. "Coyt is right there," I told them, as if they needed to be told. "Why is it that our school, with so many different cultures, including gay kids, does not think equity is important?"

After the meeting, Sharon and Melanie attempted to form an Equity Committee that would have an impact on the curriculum, but none of the other teachers at Sylvia Avenue showed any willingness to join. Melanie says, "Nobody wanted to have any part or discussion about equity. So it was just left because I think teachers did not want to be harassed by other teachers, so they just stayed away from this whole idea of equity."

The significance of this defeat cannot be overstated. Institutional support, from colleagues and from the administration, for doing classroom work that makes for a safe and inclusive educational experience for LGBTQ students is among the most important keys to its implementation. This finding is confirmed by the Every Teacher Project, a national study on LGBTQ-inclusive education that involved almost 3,400 teachers, counsellors, and other educators in the K–12 Canadian school system and was conducted in 2013–14 (survey) and 2014–15 (interviews and focus groups).[1] What it shows is that a perceived lack of institutional support from the principal and vice-principal, as well as other teachers, keeps many teachers from incorporating inclusive education into their classrooms.

A lack of resources and training is also cited as a largely significant cofactor. It is extremely interesting that teachers at faith-based schools do not cite their own religious beliefs or the religious culture of schools as the reason for not undertaking inclusive education. They, too, cite a lack of institutional support. In fact, at faith-based schools, the vast majority of teachers agree that doing inclusive education for LGBTQ students is a necessary effort that they support. Overall, the vast majority of teachers at all schools support the idea of LGBTQ-inclusive education, but only half practise it.

Bringing Safety as Equity into the Classroom

Lots of students come to Sharon's class during lunch because she will let them use the computer. Sharon explains to me that the students feel safer in her classroom than in the cafeteria or in the area outside the school.

Continuing the activity about race that she started earlier, Sharon turns to the class. "Okay, let's discuss school safety. What are we told will keep us safe? You don't have to use hands." One student shouts, "Lanyards." Sharon writes "lanyard" on the board. Other answers produce a list that Sharon writes vertically on the board:

- lanyard (ID tag)
- security guards
- police
- cameras
- rules

"What safe school policies do we have?" Sharon asks. One student yells out, "The law." There is general laughter, comments such as "you would know," and more laughter.

Sharon moves to a different blackboard. "Okay, let's make another list. What are we told about equity?" There is absolute silence in the classroom. Sharon repeats the question. One student ventures, "Muslim prayer on Friday." Sharon writes down the one response on the board. She asks, "Anything else? Okay, then, what equity policies do we have?" A tall black male student, named Wayne, whom I have noticed never takes off his coat, says, "There is no equity. It's garbage." This gets the ball rolling, and several answers are shouted at once: "Dress code." "No hats." "No nothing." "Black students are stopped more."

If there are gay students in the classroom, they are silent. Nobody mentions the needs of gay students. Sharon listens until there are no further suggestions for the list, and then she asks, "And is that equity?" Wayne answers again: "*Here* it is. Equity is shit."

Later, I talk with Melanie in her classroom during a spare period. Students have gathered in the room in the same way they do in Sharon's classroom. When I ask her whether the students are required to wear the lanyard in gym class, she yells over to one of the students, "Do you have to wear the lanyard in phys ed?" There are a lot of cries of "No, Miss." She turns to me. "And in tech, I think. They wear an apron in tech."

We sit at the back of the classroom. The walls of her classroom are bare. "I've stopped having the battles that Sharon's having with the administration. I prefer to operate under the radar."

I show her some pamphlets I've found around the school. She flips through them as she speaks. "'Your Record Doesn't End When You Turn 18.' I won't have this stuff in here. Such threats, eh? Stay in line now or you'll pay for it later."

She sighs. "In a practical way, if there are no models for the kids to show them how important it is to respect differences, then they don't learn that. What does this tell them about who they are – and about who anybody is?" Melanie fears that the negativity instilled in some students as a result of how the school treats them could lead to intolerance of other students, particularly gay students.

Before speaking again, Melanie looks at every one of the flyers, posters, and pamphlets I've collected.

In the English curriculum, if you look at it, it calls for all of these things, right? To teach the children the differences. But there's one thing you teach someone out of a book from words. And then practically, you show them a different example. So in one way, yes, the kids did programs on same-sex marriage and debates on it and so on – but the kids still, in practice, will go against it, with homosexuality, because politically, in their own lives, they know it's not the accepted thing. The same thing with equity. We study all kinds of things on equity in every curriculum and in every subject. But there's no equity in the school or in the classroom.

Tapping her finger on the booklet titled "Your Record Doesn't End When You Turn 18," Melanie makes one final comment: "So I think what we teach and what we practise are two different things."

Safety as Security: Trimble Collegiate Institute

Lorna Gillespie and Sharon Dominick are good friends – in part because they used to work together at Trimble Collegiate Institute before Sharon voluntarily transferred to Sylvia Avenue. Lorna reflects on Sharon's decision to transfer: "I think she wanted to cut down on the amount of time she was commuting every day." Lorna also considers the result of Sharon's transfer: "Sylvia Avenue is an awful place. I wish Sharon would come back here. Sylvia Avenue is all about controlling the students. We're not that bad here, but we do focus on security more than equity." Trimble Collegiate is, in the words of each student I meet, "a very multicultural" school, with high percentages of students who are black, Muslim, and of Asian and Russian descent.

Lorna tells me that the high composition of multiracial students makes it impossible for the administration to try to control identity "like they do at Sylvia Avenue." But at the same time, because of the racial composition of the school, "safety definitely means security here," she points out.

Trimble Collegiate is equipped with cameras in each hallway. Insofar as there is a dress code, the policy is not as strict as at some schools, certainly not as strict as at Sylvia Avenue, but "hats are out." Each of the students I meet tells me that there is one reason for the "no hats" policy: "So the cameras can see your face."

What Students Say about It

Len

Len is a seventeen-year-old gay student in Grade 12. He tells me that there are "forty-four cameras watching the school, inside and out." When I ask him how he knows how many cameras there are, he laughs. "We all know."

The first day I met Len, he was wearing a pink lacrosse shirt and sunglasses. His hair, looking shiny and wet, was swept up to a severe point over the middle of his forehead. As he approached me in the hallway, he said "hello" and immediately commented on his own appearance. "I dress like this – with the shades, the hair, and the expensive shoes – because I'm in Grade 12, because I'm old enough to get away with it. You can't in Grade 9 or even 11."

Once we settle into a classroom to talk, I ask him about equity programs in the school, and he is quick to answer: "There is no equity here." Len concedes that the school celebrates Black History Month and Asian Awareness Month "but only because the board makes us, and then you never hear of it again the rest of the year." There is not, in his opinion, much other "critical race work" being done.

In addition to Len, I speak with four other gay or lesbian students at this school. Once again, it strikes me that these students are more aware of the role of equity in schools than other students. Len tells me why:

> I think queer kids, particularly, understand the power of equity and what it can do, but that's the history of gays and lesbians in Ontario, isn't it? We've studied the history of the Human Rights Code and getting sexual orientation included. Look at how that changed space.[2] It allowed queers to fill up public space in a way they hadn't before. Same with the Charter and same-sex marriage.[3] So I think there's an awareness there.

These students each feel the problem of emphasizing security over equity. Schools that do so remain places where, for LGBTQ students struggling

Am I Safe Here?

with their identity, self-actualization is not encouraged or possible. For these students, and many others, this may be why safety is conceptualized in terms of equity. They perceive lack of self-actualization as the most constant threat to the integrity of their "queerness."

When I ask whether there is queer content in any of the courses at Trimble Collegiate, Len tells me that only in Lorna's class is there any significant attempt to incorporate LGBTQ content. "Sex ed is just reproduction and that's it."

According to Len, he and another student attempted to establish the school's first gay-straight alliance, but

> the administration put the kibosh on it. It doesn't fit with their idea of safety for gays, the idea that lesbians and gay students need to find each other and themselves. Safety in numbers, safety in knowing who you are, so you can protect that. Safety is more than just making sure you don't get a kick in the nuts.

Katie

Lorna introduces me to Katie, one of her Grade 12 students. Katie has flair, a love of art, and a singular way of making her queer presence known. I'm struck by the method she has fashioned not just to declare herself in Lorna's classroom but also to assert her identity more publicly. Katie has put her work up in art displays at the front entrance of the school.

Employing a simple but understated technique, Katie's artistic scheme articulates a solitary, resistant voice among what she calls the "heterosexist shouts of the crowd around me." Katie's artwork consists of her name, executed in the colours of the freedom rainbow, repeated over and over. "'I'm here and I'm queer,' as the saying goes," Katie says when she explains the purpose behind her eponymous art. "My name is Katie – and it's right next to the football trophies."

Another Mark on the Wall: Pushing the Borders of the Conception of Safety

At Trimble Collegiate, Lorna and a number of her students repudiate the invisibility forced upon LGBTQ students, choosing to be heard in the face of forces that command silence. Discrimination and oppression by

"Katie," by Katie, Trimble Collegiate Institute

silence and invisibility – the general failure even to be contemplated – has a long history among LGBTQ persons. Lorna is continually "getting into hot water" with the administration over her attempts to push the borders of her school's conception of safety on behalf of LGBTQ visibility. Lorna battles the "confines of the administrative approach to safety." This stance often means tussles with the administration. And it has sometimes caused the administration to take disciplinary action against her and required the intervention of the teachers' union.

The walls of Lorna's classroom are awash with graffiti. But unlike the urban scrawl most high schools try to avoid, Lorna encourages it.

Am I Safe Here?

She wants her students to "take ownership of the school" by expressing themselves directly on her walls.

She tells me, "The problem is just that students do not have pride of ownership, pride of place. They find themselves in a space dominated by security measures. So I decided a few years ago to open things up." Lorna's approach brought her into direct conflict with the school's principal.

Lorna sees a distinct difference between her school and Sharon's school, "where safety means controlling the students' identities." Acknowledging that the administration at Trimble Collegiate is "all about security and nothing about equity," Lorna wants to ensure that student identities remain uninhibited by the school's security concerns. She tells me, "The question of how to make a school safe is not a matter of security alone." She is determined that there be a space where students feel connected to their schools and not alienated by the very policies – or at least the interpretation of the policies – the administration enforces to protect them. Hence, she came up with the idea of the "student-identity walls." Lorna encourages all students to "take ownership" but admits she particularly encourages LGBTQ students to "stake a claim" to the walls. Len agrees: "It's a way of resisting what's going on in other parts of the school."

When word of the "student-identity walls" spread to the principal's office, the principal ordered Lorna to stop giving the students permission to "deface" the school. The principal insisted that the "graffiti" be painted over with yellow paint. Lorna responded by filing a grievance against the principal. And for three years, while the grievance was being processed, the principal was not permitted to speak with her.

As an eventual compromise, the principal agreed to have the walls covered with a removable clear plastic sheet so that no painting occurred on the walls themselves but on the covering plastic. Lorna chuckled recounting the story to me.

> So now the room is covered in artwork that is actually on clear plastic
> that's affixed to the wall, which could be removed, but after a while, even
> that she [the principal] objected to. Her complaint was that this kind of
> artwork encouraged graffiti on the rest of the school. So back we went
> at it. So the deal I finally struck with her was that the plastic could stay,

Student-identity walls at Trimble Collegiate Institute

but if I saw anyone who was marking up the walls inappropriately in other parts of the school, then I would agree to report them to the office. But I would have done that anyway.

Safety as Equity: Burton School

Delores Kent, a teacher at Burton School, gives me a copy of the course outline for the school's gay and lesbian studies course (which Lazy Daisy and I talked about in Chapter 1). "We do it every year," Dolores says. The course covers movies, literature, poetry, and media, and it includes queer artists, perspectives, and history. I ask her who takes the course. Her answer: "Anybody who wants to."

Gay and Lesbian Studies Course Outline, Burton School

Course Description: This course will focus on gay, lesbian, bisexual, trans-gendered and transsexual issues. These include position in society in the past and present, contributions to humanity historically and now, the fight for equity and contemporary issues of importance. We will investigate and discuss concepts of gender and gender identity, sexual preference and sexual expression in the context of patriarchy and its values, which permeate our culture. Health and body image issues will be explored as well as the lives of individual gay, lesbian, bisexual and transgendered people who have appeared in history.

Units

Unit 1   Introduction

Definitions	Gender	Socialization
Education	Media Portrayals	

Unit 2   Biography
GBLT people in history, politics, science, the arts and literature.

Unit 3   Political History
Homophile Movement, Gay Liberation, Queen Nation
The Law and Sexual Orientation

Unit 4   Health

Body Image	Health	Sexuality
Spirituality		

Unit 5   Contemporary Issues

Gay Pride Parade	Homophobia	AIDS

Unit 6   Literature, Arts and Entertainment

Methods	Lectures	Films
Speakers	Seminars	Group Work
Film, short stories and novels by GBLT		

Student Requirements: Each student will be required to write an evaluation once a week which records intellectual and emotional awareness with respect to the previous week's course content.

Assignments	Tests	Exam
Presentation of a biography	Independent Study – Essay and Seminar	

Evaluation:

Group Work, Class participation, Attendance, Presentations	30
Tests and Assignments	15
Journal	15
Independent Study (Essay and Seminar)	20
Exam	20

70 percent of the evaluation is based on course work and 30 percent is cumulative (Exam and 50 percent of independent study unit)

The outline for Burton's gay and lesbian studies course notes that one of its goals is to emphasize "the fight for equity" by queers and the contributions of queers to history. Another teacher tells me that one of the ideas of the course is to include content that will benefit all students by introducing the concept that gender and sexuality are culturally influenced and constructed.

After reading the course outline, Lazy Daisy tells me why she thinks courses like this are important:

> Yeah, this is all really cool. I·was talking to my brother about whether he thought gay and lesbian studies should be in schools. And I was like, "Honestly, I think that the people who take the course aren't the people who need it, and it should be in the curriculum." And he's like, "Oh, well, why do I need to learn about that, you know? I'm not gay." And I'm like, "That's not the point." There just has to be general acceptance, like lessons taught early on to students, to just learn to treat everybody equally, and we need to have this kind of course for later on ... It should be taught really early on. It makes a difference to how people feel in general about queers, I think.

Alexander, a Grade 12 student, tells me his opinion of the benefits of the course: "I love it. But I just wish it was at the school I came from because they need it more."

Students at Burton School wear no lanyards and follow no dress code, yet it becomes clear from my conversations with staff and students at Burton that they think of it as a safe school. Equity is the norm. And they readily recognize how their school environment differs from schools that focus on safety as control.

What Students Say about It

Benjamin
I spend a lot of time with Benjamin, a Grade 12 student. He attributes the climate of Burton School to its small size and, more importantly, to the fact that both the teachers and the students want the school to be a

place that not only focuses on equity but, compared with most other schools, is also "more socially active – like Coyt."

In describing Burton's environment, Benjamin makes several comparisons to other schools in the neighbourhood; Sylvia Avenue and Coyt are nearby, and students are well aware of the differences between them. Benjamin describes Sylvia Avenue as "threatening" and "not safe." I ask him and Lazy Daisy whether this is true for all students or just LGBTQ students. They agree that Sylvia Avenue would not be a good school for any student but add that, for LGBTQ youth, it would be unbearable. Benjamin explains, "I don't think there are any out students at Sylvia Avenue. It's funny how the three schools are so close to each other and so different. Sylvia Avenue is all about being a prison. Coyt is like paradise, or that's what they think, and we're kind of more like Coyt, but not as much." When I ask Benjamin to describe his school, he says,

> It's like a little hippie commune. That's the way I like to think of it, anyway. It's pretty cool. Everyone here adheres to – even if they didn't, like, know it beforehand – a pretty open and accepting way about their day. There is no violence. There is no real homophobia, and the culture is cool for queers. Anything that's said and not liked is discussed versus just being dealt with authoritarian-style.

The other distinguishing characteristic of Burton School is that it comprises only Grades 11 and 12. Benjamin explains to me how students are admitted to Burton School:

> You have to venture here versus being assigned from your previous middle school. You make a point of finding it. Before coming here, I went to "Crappy Collegiate." I wasn't being academically challenged and, socially, there wasn't much there for me. You get immune to walking the halls and being called a faggot every day, but you also get bored of it. You'd like a different experience.

When I ask Benjamin whether there are rules in place at Burton School that specifically target safety and control behaviour to reduce bullying, he insists, "There are none. You can do whatever you like so long as it's not offensive, and I've never seen anyone tread the line of offensiveness, personally. But you see, it's different here because they focus on equity."

Benjamin corrects himself, telling me that there is, in fact, one very strict rule at his school: "We're not welcome in Sylvia Avenue. They're not allowed to come here, and we're not allowed to go there. Same with Coyt. But I think the rule is really in place to keep the students from Sylvia Avenue out of Burton and Coyt. That's really what it's for."

Benjamin tells me that Burton uses Sylvia Avenue's gym but is permitted to do so only at 7:00 on Monday mornings. Burton School's students are expected to show up, use the gym and showers, and leave before the Sylvia Avenue students arrive. Benjamin, Lazy Daisy, and all of the students at Burton School who speak with me take pains to tell me that their school is "nothing like" Sylvia Avenue. As I discovered, the students at Sylvia Avenue readily agree with that assessment. Students at each of these schools possess a clear understanding of how their schools differ in governing and how each school is perceived by the others.

Celebrating, Not Just Tolerating

Benjamin explains to me that Burton School is trying to be more proactive about its equity policies: "Right now we're kind of pro-equity, but we're trying to be more socially active." He hands me one of the "Celebrate Diversity" stickers that he has been putting up all over his school. "For me, these stickers are more about the *celebrate* part than the *diversity* part. I'm tired of being tolerated – I want to be celebrated."

For many gay and lesbian adults, the right to get married was the last hurdle in Canada for gay rights. For the queer youth I meet at the different schools, celebration and participation seem less about any single identifiable cultural signpost, such as marriage, than about having their lives and their realities recognized and celebrated. Nor does safety mean just being left alone, either.

Benjamin believes his school could do a better job. He feels that Coyt creates a more inclusive environment than his own school: "Our school is pretty damned good, but Coyt probably does more." When I ask Benjamin in what ways his school is trying to be more like Coyt, he

Am I Safe Here?

impresses me with the breadth of what the students and teachers in his school are actually doing:

> We actually are a pretty socially active school right now. We do a lot of fundraising for charity. A fashion show just went by on Thursday – I basically spearheaded it, really – and we raised over five hundred bucks for AIDS charities. We have an active boycott against Coca Cola because of their union practices in South America. Most recently, we don't like Walmart. Christmastime, we do these huge bags for women's shelters. That's something I'm big into. Even though every single person doesn't participate, the fact that we do these things sets a tone for the culture here and brings some sense of goals outside of academia, if you will. But dress codes, and lanyards, and rules about how to behave? No, no, no. Not ever.

Benjamin admits that student commitment to these kinds of endeavours "changes every semester," but he assures me that, as far as he knows, "there's always something going on." He explains that "it depends on the students and the teachers, but it's pretty cool. We have zero violence because we have zero hate. It's really a culture that makes queers, everybody, safe and sound, so we can think outside the school."

Safety as Social Justice: Elizabeth Coyt Alternative School

Visiting Coyt, you cannot help but come away wishing this had been your high school. It is difficult to imagine anyone not feeling this way. Coyt offers a full range of high school grades, 9 through 12, for its five hundred students. Like Burton School, Coyt is near Sylvia Avenue, and students from each of the schools are prohibited from trespassing on the other's property.

Benjamin speculated that this "no trespass" rule is really aimed at the students of Sylvia Avenue, and each of the students I speak to at Coyt agrees. Carla, a Grade 12 student at Coyt, explains, "We are technically not allowed in Sylvia Avenue, but it's more about Sylvia Avenue coming into our school – or going into Burton School. The idea is to keep the students from Sylvia Avenue out of Burton and Coyt."

There are numerous ways that equity can be put to work to promote safety in schools. Burton School and Coyt are models for these approaches. In a most striking way, Coyt conceives of safety not only in terms of equity but also, more proactively, in terms of safety as social justice. "Yeah, social justice," Carla fairly beams at me. She is proud of Coyt and happy to be here.

> We're all about being proactive here, and we think in terms of social justice, not just equity, which I think our school feels is more about acknowledging or appreciating diversity. It's an open-catchment school, so anyone across the city can go, but we all wear uniforms. We want to avoid all that stuff with brand labels – and it just takes that whole level of pressure out for being in a high school, so it is a high school that focuses on promoting equity and social justice, and it's a totally cool, comfortable environment. We refer to all our teachers by their first names, so it's a really friendly, really open environment.

For students at Coyt, this conception of safety as a matter of social justice is the ideal model for all schools.

What Students Say about It

Carla and Emma

Carla is a terrific speaker. She is articulate, energetic, and happy to talk about her school. She seems to be happy generally and to be a very friendly, caring individual. Carla is about to graduate and has attended Coyt for four years. She speaks glowingly of the school's social justice philosophy:

> I think it's become so ingrained in the culture of the school, you almost take it for granted. It's just the way it is – probably in the way that at most schools, it's exactly the way it *isn't*. It's a great school. Here, there's more emphasis on establishing a culture rather than [on] responding to what students do, but not doing anything else the rest of the time.

Carla's favourite subject is film and video. The course gave her the chance to take the school's social justice concerns to the streets outside the school:

I decided to go around the city and video all the hetero stuff I could find to show how heterodominant our culture is, sort of to intervene and say, to anybody who would see my video, wait a minute here. You were talking about what makes schools safer for queer kids before – I think seeing that kind of video does.

It is not difficult to see why Carla points to the heteronormative culture as worthy of attention. The LGBTQ students in this book consistently make the point that there is no such thing as an isolated homophobic moment of harassment or bullying, only the inevitable consequences of being queer in a culture, or a school, that makes no space for it. Coyt, however, actively combats homophobia while celebrating and making space for different sexualities on many fronts. The school attempts to do this in many ways. I was struck that many of them were initiatives in which students played key roles.

Over the Rainbow

Over the Rainbow is the driving force in the school. Even its name distinguishes this group from other gay-straight alliances. Carla tells me, "We have Over the Rainbow, which is a big, big group at our school, which basically says, 'We're past *Are you homophobic?* We're just getting on to *Okay, we've accepted it*. Now we'll deal with the issues and try and promote queerness within our school and, of course, the community.'"

Carla's girlfriend, Emma, is also in Grade 12 at Coyt. When I met them, they had been dating for over a year. Carla and Emma held hands whenever I met them at the school and sometimes kissed in the hallways. Neither would do so, however, outside the school or when they were near Sylvia Avenue. "Not safe to do that near Sylvia Avenue," Emma tells me. "A guy and a girl threw a can of pop at us when we walked by there once, so we've never done it again." Emma agrees that Over the Rainbow is more than a "regular" GSA:

We have Over the Rainbow but that's kind of a different sort of thing. Not that all GSAs are the same, but Over the Rainbow is not like any GSA I've ever heard of. For one thing, it's not about combating homophobia. That's just not there at this school. In fact, you definitely get a little marginalized if you are homophobic, so you learn very quickly to keep it to yourself. I really don't know of anyone who would say anything homophobic. And besides, Over the Rainbow is more like an entire student council or government. It really runs things here.

Emma tells me that Over the Rainbow posters are put up all over the school to promote the group's events. She has never known them to be defaced. Her favourite poster reads, "I'm straight but it might be a phase."

"Another really good one," she tells me, "says, 'Why in this society are we more comfortable with two men holding guns than holding hands?'"

But all the students I speak with agree that Over the Rainbow's best known achievement is Unite, an annual multimedia conference celebrating sexuality. Emma explains the impact of Over the Rainbow on the entire school and the significance of Unite as a school-wide unifying event to which other schools in the city are invited:

> We do Unite every year, almost every year, which is a conference that usually involves sexuality and art of many forms like film or photography. And lots of schools come, but it's not open to the public. Over the Rainbow really affects all parts of school life. We didn't get to do [Unite] this year because two teachers who really do a lot for it were away this year, but last year, we did ... There were at least five hundred people here. Unite is celebrating sexuality in art. It's a fairly broad topic. There is queer content, but it speaks to everybody. It is really cool and it was a lot of fun to organize.

The notion of promoting equity as social justice – the difference between equity and diversity, on the one hand, and social justice, on the other – is an important theme that each person at Coyt underscores without prompting from me. Carla tells me that "Over the Rainbow is about what the school is about."

Emma agrees: "Over the Rainbow is about sexuality and gender issues and just letting people blossom. We're so past just acknowledging and tolerating differences." When I press Emma for details, she says,

We do tons of stuff. We have a policy of sexual harassment that's in there – this cannot be done, that cannot be done. We spent a little too long talking to the equity department at [the school board], talking about changing the "Mother and Father" on forms, just lots of stuff like that. Reshaping on paper how families have changed now, for instance. And, of course, we do tons of stuff for AIDS all the time.

Emma and Carla take me around the school to look at one of a number of displays dealing with AIDS awareness and education. When I ask whether there are "Safe Space" posters around the school, Carla assures me there are but adds, "That's the smallest thing we do." I'm reminded of Gabe Picard in Thunder Bay and the administration's view that its own proposal to settle his human rights complaint with a single "Safe Space" sign was an enormous undertaking. I tell Emma and Carla about Gabe's story. Carla responds, "You can see how far schools have to go, the range of responses that are possible to making safe space for queers. In that case, it's just making excuses. If you compare that with what we do, you can see what's really required."

Girls and Boys Come Out to Play

When I ask Carla whether she has ever heard of any bullying or verbal harassment of LGBTQ students at Coyt, her answer is decisive: "Nope. I've had, I think, maybe two passing comments in the first years of high school, but that was *outside* the school, and there was one from students of another school nearby just in passing. Okay, it was Sylvia Avenue."

I wonder whether the incoming students in Grade 9 are respectful of sexual diversity. Emma tells me,

Now that's a little bit different, especially the Grade 9 and 10 boys. Yes, I should mention that. They do call each other *fag* when they get here, but the seniors do smack them over the head, quite literally sometimes. Boys saying, "This project is so gay." The phrase "That's so gay" is also in there a lot with boys. Generally, if a student says that, someone turns on their heel and lectures them for about an hour.

At every school I visit, the students and teachers, males and females, acknowledge a difference between how gay boys and gay girls are regarded. Even with the apparent accomplishments of day-to-day life at Coyt, I wonder whether this disparity survives even here. Emma talks about the more overt demands directed at boys:

> I think boys and girls are both definitely being monitored by other students, but it's much more out there for boys. There was one incident where another school was here for an "improv" competition. We have a big improv team, so we held the improv semifinals at our school. We had one school verbally harass my friend Cal for being gay. He came into the room as he usually does and went, "Ta da!" And they kind of coughed under their breath and yelled out, "Hey look, it's a fag!" And everyone from our school just kind of went, "Excuse me?" So we all got up and, boy, were those students ever not happy because we turned around on them, and it was not a good thing.

Students as Part of the Solution

I wonder how Coyt *would* respond to an incident of verbal or physical harassment. "It would probably be mediation," Emma suggests. "And the principal would probably talk to both parties separately and try to figure out what happened, and there would be *some* punishment. I believe physical harassment is a serious suspension at least. But really, I can't imagine that ever *happening* here."

Benjamin at Burton School has told me that as progressive as Burton School tries to be, there are no gay books in its library. At Coyt there are many. Carla tells me that a group of students from Over the Rainbow went up and down the shelves in the library placing rainbow stickers on the spines of any books with gay content or written by gay authors.

Carla says, "We also have stickers for African studies, we have stickers for French studies, feminist studies, we've got a huge range, so we decided to do it for queer content, too." Emma remembers that "in the span of two months, I did queer theory in English, queer film in videography, and an essay on queer theory in English again."

Several months earlier, I interviewed two transgender students at two different Toronto high schools. When I ask Emma whether the climate of

Coyt would be likely to accommodate a transgender student, she says, "It would probably be noticed, especially since we're a small school and you see almost everyone in the halls, but I don't think it would be noticed negatively necessarily because we're generally very supportive of each other. The important thing is that we have a culture here that can make room for somebody like that." Emma reminds me of Over the Rainbow's influence: "Our kind of motto is 'It's assumed that we're over being homophobic. Let's move on to something bigger.'"

Of all the surprising ways at Coyt that students contribute to the social justice atmosphere – and there are many – nothing surprises me more than what Emma tells me about the school's "sex ed" course and the issue of Grade 9 students:

> This year we're planning to take over Grade 9 sex ed. Over the Rainbow, yeah. Actually, seniors in general have decided that it's really no good because it's [district-]written curriculum and, of course, there's no queer content. Or if there is, it's kind of mumbled somewhere in there, so we've decided to go in and teach the class. The admin has to approve, and they have for next year.

I ask Emma whether there is any way that Coyt could be improved upon for LGBTQ students. "Not really," she tells me. "I mean, I came out in Grade 10 and the response was, 'Didn't you tell us that already?' Oh, I thought, okay. In some ways, I wish there was sort of more reaction."

I ask if there is anything else she wants to tell me about Coyt. "Absolutely fantastic is the only thing I can say."

Cal

I ask to meet Cal, the student who was called a fag at the improv competition. Emma and Carla have told me they adore Cal. The students at Coyt strike me as carrying with them a secure sense of self – Cal gives off the same confident energy. The first thing Cal wants me to know is that his school is "great." The first thing I want to hear about is the incident at the improv semifinals. But I decide to let the subject come up on its own. I begin by asking Cal to tell me why Coyt is great and what makes it special and different from other schools, particularly Burton School. He explains,

> It's really open. We are very liberal, and we try to include all different types of religion and cultures and sexualities. The teachers are really great. If you just need to talk or something, they're really willing to make some time in their schedule. They just listen to whatever you need to say. And students are like that, too. It's the whole environment here. The upper-year students really notice the lower-year students, and I think if you're in Grade 9 or 10, you value that. That's a pretty important part of the school, in my opinion.
>
> There's about five hundred or six hundred students here, and we're [very close to] Burton School and Sylvia Avenue. And it's interesting because those are very different schools. I mean, Burton School is more like us, but it's still quite different. So we don't usually do a lot of stuff together because we are so different.

Over the Rainbow and Social Activism

I press Cal for details on the differences between Burton and Coyt, and the first subject he raises is Over the Rainbow:

> We have a group called Over the Rainbow, which is not a GSA – it's a group that is very open in teaching about sexuality, but all over the school. You have to know about Over the Rainbow to understand our school.
>
> And two years now, we've held Unite. We reach out to different schools in the [district], and we invite a couple students from each high school to come here. And we have a bunch of different queer artists and musicians, and also different speakers during the year who just come in and talk to students about different things. It doesn't have to be about actual sexuality but just doing art and making music and stuff. We didn't get to do Unite this year because one of our teachers who is key to it is out of the country.

When I ask Cal what would happen to a student at the school who had no interest in Over the Rainbow, he tells me that there is no way to

Am I Safe Here?

get away from Over the Rainbow. But he can't imagine that anyone would want to do that. Cal confirms what Emma, Carla, and others have told me about the group's influence extending to the entire school. He speaks extensively about the school's "social activism":

> We've got a Guatemala project, which is where we're working on helping out people in Guatemala. So they're selling coffee beans, and all the money goes to help people who are losing land because of deforestation. They're losing businesses and stuff. And we just have so many different groups. It's hard to just name all of them. We have an animal rights group. A group that works for AIDS awareness and support for PWAs [people with AIDS]. We've got a couple of those, in fact. We're quite into being aware of globalization and HIV/AIDS work.

A Different Kind of Dress Code

There is a school uniform at Coyt. The students I meet here do not seem to mind wearing it. However, I have a difficult time discerning the requirements of the dress policy. I don't see any American Eagle or Hollister or A&F T-shirts in evidence, but the range of acceptable "dress" seems very broad. Cal gives me the specifics:

> It just has to be any of the school colours, really, so white, hunter green, maroon, or navy blue. A button-up shirt or a rugby shirt is fine. Really any kind of shirt, so long as it's those colours and no brand names. And we just have to wear blue pants or a blue kilt or a skirt. Any kind of socks and any kind of shoes, really. So that's probably why you're not seeing a school uniform per se.

I wonder whether Cal or any of the students feel that a school uniform or dress code is an attempt to control student identity. Have the students ever rebelled against the dress code? Cal tells me,

> Oh, no, because there's no sense that's the overall scheme of things here. Our dress policy is about doing something for equality, part of a social justice approach, so when it's given to you that way, you don't feel you're being controlled. We're trying to eradicate social status with it.

I know that in different schools you go to, it's very ... you have to have name-brand clothing to be cool. You have to have this and you have to have that. And our uniforms just kind of cut away from all that because you can't really wear that stuff. So it's just everyone is equal because everyone's wearing the same stuff. It's part of being equal.

I ask whether the administration, or anyone else, has ever suggested that there are security reasons for having a dress policy in place. Cal muses, "I guess there ... could be. I mean the teachers can figure out more easily if someone's not supposed to be in the school, if that person doesn't have a uniform. But it's not the primary thing. It's more equality."

Boys Beware

I ask Cal whether all students in all years embrace the school's underlying philosophies. He agrees they do, but like Emma, he also mentions the Grade 9 boys and the issue of dealing with masculinity. Just as Emma told me about the seniors' takeover of sex ed as a partial response to the needs of the incoming students, Cal tells me about another school project that developed out of the same concerns. Cal's videography class was instrumental in producing a school movie. A school movie, Cal explains, is like a school play "except that it's a movie." This year the movie, which was written and directed by students and performed by students of all grades, was called *Boys Beware*. Cal tells me, "It's a gay-themed piece dealing with masculinity and dealing with the issue of the incoming boys."

This is a theme that is raised at every school. Without exception, every student and teacher I speak to tells me – sometimes reluctantly, not wishing to contribute to a hierarchy of oppression – that gay male students have it toughest in schools because of straight boys. Carla has already brought up this subject and provided me with her assessment of the difference:

Just because this society is so masculinist, it's a lot harder for boys to come out because they're worried about what their guy friends will think. Masculinity rules. Meanwhile, for girls, it's like, "Okay, good." Because girls are allowed to be sensitive and touchy. And for a lot of guys, they're interested in two girls being together, but not two boys together.

Cal's take on the distinction is similar:

I think straight men prefer seeing two women – they're okay with that because it's hot or whatever – two women having sex. Whereas two guys having sex is totally gross and disgusting in this culture.

I know one or two people who are in Grade 9 who are just like, "It would be okay for lesbians, but it's not okay for gay boys." I'm like, "Why? What's the difference?" Obviously, that kind of cultural bias expresses itself in expected ways.

Safe Space

When I ask Cal whether there are any spaces in the school where he feels safer or less safe than he does in other spaces, he returns to the subject of Burton School and Sylvia Avenue:

I feel safe pretty much all over the school. Going into Sylvia Avenue is kind of a creepy thing. And our auditorium is half Sylvia Avenue, half ours. So going into that area, there's Sylvia Avenue students allowed to be there, of course. So it's kind of weird going there. We can use their gym in the morning, but I think it's kind of scary going into Sylvia Avenue, especially for gay guys.

We don't do a lot with Burton School. I don't actually know a lot about Burton, either, but it's not scary. When I said I was going to come here, my mum was worried about Sylvia Avenue. Burton we didn't really question.

I've never had a problem with anyone from Sylvia Avenue. They've never harassed me or anything, but I've heard stories. I don't want to judge.

He adds,

In this school, you're safe no matter what you are or who you are here. If anything were to happen, the entire teacher-student body would just be on that person *like that*. It's just so open, and if anyone had an issue or something, they'd just be in the office. But I can't really even imagine it.

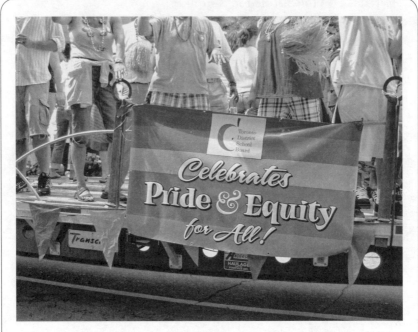

Toronto District School Board "Pride & Equity" float

I mean, we help organize Pride Prom, which is kind of like a prom for students from other schools who are too afraid to take their partner or whatever to their actual dance. It's held at Buddies in Bad Times Theatre. We help decorate and we help come up with a theme.

And every year we walk in the Pride Parade. It says, "Toronto District School Board," but it's usually mainly us. We work very differently than other schools and things. We just finished doing a literary project on queer theory. Me and a couple of my friends, we did one. And we did a project on homosexuality in the media.

In fact, some months later, I looked for students from Coyt at the Pride Parade, and sure enough, they walked in the parade carrying banners promoting equity and rode on the "Pride & Equity" float. Their anti-bullying posters and pro-equity signs elicited enthusiastic applause from the crowds as they moved along the streets of Toronto.

Am I Safe Here?

School Safety Put into Practice

Still thinking of the improv incident, I ask Cal what would happen if someone in the school called him a fag. He explains,

> Half the student body would go up to them. There's just so many people that would respond to that on their own. It's just like, I know one time, we actually had an improv competition, and we had a couple of other students from other schools here. Well, they called me a fag. And my entire improv team ... that other team was just totally blacklisted – that entire team. We all ended up beating them. It was good.
>
> They were still allowed to compete, and we were debating telling the coach. We were debating telling the people actually running the improv games. But it really upset some of my teammates because they knew that if I had been black and they called me the "n" word – I don't really want to say it – that the team would've been off. But because of the society we live in right now, it's not really as punishable, I guess. People think they can do it.
>
> Sometimes the Grade 9s here will do that, say things, just because they're not used to it around here. But then, by Grade 10, they're completely open to it. So it just shows you, you can change it.

I ask Cal whether he has any views on how going to school could be improved for LGBTQ students at *other* schools since he shares Emma's high opinion of his own school. He replies,

> I think just ... really cutting down on the harassment and stuff by having a place where it doesn't happen in the first place. Making sure that the students aren't getting beaten up, or verbally harassed, or cyberbullied, or whatever. You have to start with that because that's what's going on in schools now.
>
> Making it safer for them and just trying to get the teachers involved and making it part of the whole school. Because there's even some teachers that can be homophobic. But mostly, more education on the subject. Really trying to get it into people's heads that this is an okay thing. Really being a social activist because just getting involved after something happens doesn't deal with what gays need to be safer.

Coyt is not interested merely in intervening in a bullying event after it occurs. Neither is the school concerned with controlling students' identities or emphasizing security. Cal describes Coyt's view of safety like this:

> The school is about social justice on *all* fronts. Not just queer stuff, but there's certainly an emphasis on queer content – not just fighting homophobia but doing more than that, making spaces safe for queer kids when they show up in Grade 9 or transfer in. So I would say safety at this school is about being active and making this a space where problems just don't happen in the first place.

Cal's vision of schools supports what I heard from Emma and Carla: merely intervening when LGBTQ students are harassed or threatened does not address their conceptions of feeling safe. When I ask Cal to speculate about what it must be like for LGBTQ students at other schools who do not have this kind of environment, he says, "I think that there would be a fear all the time and a sense that it wasn't safe. There would likely be more bullying, more harassment. There probably is. I know we have none here." The experience of Gabe Picard and the solitary "Safe Space" sign seems far removed from how safety is put into practice at Coyt.

Summing Up

For many LGBTQ students, schools are not places of learning or even social development but places where they are abused and terrorized and oppressed for being different. This oppression takes more forms than "generic" bullying. LGBTQ students perceive their safety to be threatened in ways that may be different from the experience of heterosexual students. Whereas heterosexual students may fail to see their use of "that's so gay" as anything other than innocuous, LGBTQ students and their allies react to the expression as a constant reminder that their security is under threat and their safety tenuous.

LGBTQ students are united in their view that safety must be considered broadly to include measures that promote equity and inclusiveness in the education system. Students' own views of what would make a safe school often differ from how their own schools go about constructing safety.

The students themselves suggest four categories for how schools deliver or conceptualize safety, along a spectrum: (1) schools that see safety in terms of security and try to *control* student identities, (2) schools that emphasize *security* but with less strict measures of control than those at the end of the spectrum, (3) schools that focus on *equity* as a means of ensuring student safety, and (4) schools that go even further than equity to consider *social justice* aims.

For schools practising *equity* and *social justice*, students play a central role in school governance and in creating and maintaining an inclusive curriculum and climate. Student connectedness is emphasized. But very few schools fall into the social justice category.

Most schools fall into either *control* or *security* categories or display elements of both. These schools see safety in terms of controlling or taming a threatening student body. At these schools, the emphasis is on security guards, surveillance cameras, dress codes, and mandatory student and teacher ID badges, or lanyards.

However, schools do not necessarily fall neatly into one classification. A school that is generally considered to emphasize security, or even control of student identities through measures like dress codes, may also have elements of equity or social justice. But these are sporadic pockets because of a few committed teachers and students. For its part, Burton School, which emphasizes a commitment to safety as equity, also tips toward social justice in some ways. So the spectrum, from control to social justice, does not necessarily represent unchallengeable truths about these and other schools but is, rather, a useful means by which to view how the pursuit of safety plays out on the ground.

Not surprisingly, given their status as "other" in most schools, LGBTQ students point out that failing to emphasize equity or inclusiveness in safe school efforts marginalizes them. Mere tolerance of LGBTQ students is not a high aspiration. Such approaches produce inequities, resulting in their alienation. They do not feel safe or respected; they feel threatened. And they do not feel a connection with their schools. Why would they?

What Needs to Be Done

- Safety needs to be conceptualized broadly in order to emphasize equity and inclusive education as proactive components.
- Safe school policies must not be generically conceived but must consider the specific and individual needs of LGBTQ students.
- Safe school committees at individual schools should have diverse membership, reflecting the different backgrounds and identities of the school community.
- Policies affecting school safety should be student-focused and student-centred, with students themselves playing key roles in responses to homophobic or other forms of harassment (peer-to-peer mediation) and in implementing curriculum (students teaching other students), particularly LGBTQ-inclusive education. Disciplinary pieces in policies are necessary, but students should play a role in these responses.
- Students should lead by example, such as senior students making clear to junior students that homophobia is not cool.
- Safe and inclusive school policies must emphasize and maintain student connectedness within schools, not alienate students by treating them as the source of the threat to school safety.
- Heterosexual and other privileges, as well as social rank, need to be addressed and challenged. Curriculum must examine the social construction of the sexuality and gender of all students in order to contest cultural hierarchies rather than sustaining a normative order of gender and sexuality, as well as other privileges.

3

Homophobia, Heterosexism, and Heteronormativity

> Heteronormativity is subtle, it just runs along like
> an engine you forget is running, like sitting in your
> car and not remembering the motor is on. But the
> heterosexism of school is pretty blunt.
>
> – *Dalton, Grade 12 student, Toronto*

Both students and teachers have argued that safety must be defined broadly to emphasize equity and inclusive education approaches. *Inclusiveness* is a word that seems easily understood – but what is *equity*? What does it mean to *do equity*? What is *equity* trying to get at?

In one sense, doing equity means simply taking individual facts and circumstances into account in order to find a just solution for a particular situation. Equity focuses on the individual. With that in mind, this chapter delves more deeply into the individual circumstances and individual facts of what it means for LGBTQ students to go to school.

First of all, for most of these students, going to school means finding themselves in a school culture that assumes that all students are heterosexual. Most schools make this assumption simply by refusing to acknowledge their LGBTQ citizens. When LGBTQ students are invisible, they are certainly not included or embraced.

In fact, most LGBTQ students fear that coming out means rejection, harassment, and further isolation. They fear being discovered, being known for who they are, even as they understand their own power to transform the culture of schools by openly expressing their identity. This chapter, then, seeks to broaden the concept of bullying to the larger position of LGBTQ students in their schools. You will hear how, for many, their greater oppression comes from cultural exclusion. In this way, bullying is no longer just a generic phenomenon. In fact, bullying and harassment no longer remain divorced from cultural and ideological underpinnings but derive directly from them.

Joey's Poem

The house is restless. Diana Goundrey paces backstage, waiting for the "showstopper" she knows is coming. Diana is the guidance counsellor at Brookwood Collegiate and Vocational School. She is the person most closely allied with LGBTQ youth at this downtown school.

Joey, a black Grade II student at Brookwood, is about to take the stage. He intends to come out to his entire high school.

Brookwood is a predominantly security-oriented school. The guidance office is filled with the same booklets I found at Sylvia Avenue Collegiate and Vocational School. Pamphlets warn students about getting a criminal record. There are flyers on the Youth Criminal Justice Act.[1] The students I meet tell me there is a significant population of gang members, strippers, and self-called "deviants." Many of them are presumably sitting in the audience.

I have been to a number of student-run assemblies dealing with bullying and making schools safer. Each one feels like an "opening night." There is a sense of expectation in the air, a constant buzz of conversation. It is exhilarating and inspiring to see students organizing and participating in these events. They courageously face their peers, identifying themselves as LGBTQ youth.

Joey is quiet and thoughtful, deliberate in his conduct, and measured in his choice to come out to the entire school. What is doubly interesting and striking about Joey's announcement is that it comes not at an event organized by or in support of LGBTQ youth but at a Black History Month event. Joey takes the stage, standing before several hundred of his peers, and delivers a confident performance that will, I am sure, be re-membered by some for years.

Facing the crowded auditorium, Joey changes his life – and, he hopes, the lives of others. He chooses to read a poem he has written.

Even a brief excerpt captures how a bare stage is made majestic by Joey's presence and the force of simple words, his own:

> Life ain't all
> That peaches and cream
> For I am determined
> To fight for my dreams ...
>
> People don't understand
> The pain that I feel
> They mock and they tease
> But I have to deal ...
>
> I am strong, bold, courageous
> For I am proud to be black
> But people are unkind
> They all say I'm whack
>
> I tried to hide
> I tried to run
> But who I was pretending to be
> Just wasn't any fun ...
>
> I have come to realize ...
>
> I can't change the colour of my skin
> I can't change my hair, height or eyes
> And I can't change the fact that I am gay
> And ... *Why would I* ...?

Schooling Normal

Notwithstanding all of the gains that have been made in society in the past thirty years – and there have been enormous advances – hostility toward LGBTQ persons remains. Denial of their full citizenship is a common reality within the four walls of most schools.

For LGBTQ students, pursuing safety as equity means addressing the heteronormativity of schools, including how most schools convey dominant gender roles and heterosexist norms. They speak about the problem of articulating a gay or queer identity in high schools, pointing to a hierarchy in which the higher status of heterosexual students is consistently vouched for. LGBTQ voices are consistently discouraged and stifled.

Policy makers and safe school committees have ignored or undervalued the ways that heteronormative gender scripts are privileged in the process of schooling. All of this occurs, of course, to the detriment of LGBTQ youth, who are not only devalued but also threatened in ways that are not being considered under current policy approaches.

Dalton, a Grade 12 student at Brookwood, describes to me the normative aspects of schooling – a LGBTQ student's awareness of the systemic denial of LGBTQ voices:

> I think queer kids, generally, are probably more aware of the heterosexist nature of schools than straight kids. Anybody who is trying to get by in an oppressive atmosphere or culture would tend to be, I think ... High schools are pretty heteronormative all the way through and homophobic, for sure, particularly in the early grades. But even the students that may think they're not homophobic, there's no question that they're very heterosexist. And why would they not be, given the heteronormativity of the school in general? The curriculum, dances, clubs, the posters you see on the walls, the movies they show in class, sex ed, sports, the teachers, all of it.

Although most schools may be organized this way, the situation is not inevitable or unchangeable. Both administrators and teachers can play a role in developing *different* approaches, particularly ones that stress a broader conception of safety that includes equity and inclusiveness.

At Joey's presentation, when he comes out to his school as gay, there is an audible gasp in the audience. Then there is the inevitable murmur that ripples over a crowd when people realize something iconoclastic, even exciting, is happening. And then quiet.

Diana Goundrey, the guidance counsellor at Brookwood, interprets the audience reaction as a respectful silence. Then she laughs. "Wonderful, complicating equity. We *have* it – but it's not straightforward."

Joey is very humble about the presentation and quiet about his feelings. He does not want to talk about the experience afterward. But he is very satisfied with his contribution to the celebrations of Black History Month and with his choice to make a "gay statement."

Diana describes the experience for Joey and for the school this way:

> The issue is not a lack of well-written policies – we have those – but of other factors, one being an emphasis on law and order responses and a de-emphasis on equity and social justice. What oppresses most of these kids is the need to play it straight. Nobody's going to punch Joey out over this. But what will they be thinking? What line is drawn around him? I hope none. I think Joey occupies a certain status in the school where that won't happen. He's close to graduating, but that's not true for kids coming in the door.

The Systemic Stuff

Law and order responses are certainly necessary to dismantle the heteronormative school structure – but they're not the only thing needed. Tim McCaskell, who spent many years as an equity officer with the Toronto District School Board (TDSB), tells me, "You have to have your rules-and-consequences pieces. But you need your equity piece as well." He tells me that "the rules-and-consequences part, the part that is often being aimed at in policy discussions, is only dealing with the actions of individuals." Asked to elaborate, he puts it this way:

> Having policies around harassment and bullying is certainly not enough. You've got to have regular educational work to dismantle and constantly challenge the kinds of cultural values, the kinds of stereotypes the kids will be learning from the rest of their environment, in school and elsewhere. And you've got to have all this systemic stuff in place, not only in terms of harassment but in terms of these values being promoted. That's the situation for many schools.

However, the board policies now in the TDSB, that were won over a huge ... struggle ..., are probably, I think, the best in North America, if not anywhere. I mean they're really very, very comprehensive. There's always room for tinkering, but generally that piece is good. The problem is the implementation – it's not happening.

It is important to bear in mind the "systemic stuff" McCaskell points to. These are the cultural values and stereotypes that students learn both in official spaces like the curriculum and in unofficial spaces like school-yards and cafeterias.

The official curriculum generally lacks content about the achievements of LGBTQ historical figures or ignores their sexual orientation, as with Leonardo da Vinci and Walt Whitman, among others. At the same time, the so-called unofficial curriculum – the many ways that school culture reinforces homophobic attitudes and language – both underwrites and constitutes the homophobia being learned by students.

Many parents complain if the curriculum has a LGBTQ component. But what must be understood is that students are learning and talking about gay people, trans people, even if only unofficially, in locker rooms, on playing fields, in cafeterias, in hallways, and in smoking areas – throughout all the years they go to school.

In many ways, McCaskell's comments strike me as a direct response to a question posed rhetorically to me by Ryan, a fifteen-year-old Grade 9 student at Triangle, where all of the students are LGBTQ. It is Canada's only high school program for LGBTQ youth and describes its mission as "providing a classroom where Lesbian, Gay, Bisexual and Transgender (LGBT) youth can learn and earn credits in a safe, harassment-free, equity-based environment, and developing and teaching curriculum which includes and celebrates LGBT literature, history, persons and issues."[2] Ryan, like so many others, criticizes schools that fail to recognize and embrace their LGBTQ students:

I live with my dad. My mother left us a long time ago. When I do see her, she never asks me how I am, and you know why? Because she doesn't want to know. If she knew, she might have to do something. That's what it's like at schools. They don't want to know what's going on every day. They'll deal with physical or verbal things, but they don't want to ask you how you *are* ... What would the ramifications for school policy be if they listened to students?

On a different day, in a different conversation, Tim McCaskell provides the answer. In his view, the structure of schooling would change fundamentally if schools embraced equity and dealt with more than just the "physical or verbal things." His words are worth quoting at length:

When you're talking about a system of oppression, you've got to think of it as kind of an iceberg. You've got individual actions, and with that, there's the physical bullying, the name-calling, the beating-up piece – because of the dominant ideas. Queers are second-rate, queers are unnatural, queers are different. If a student calls somebody a fag, they get hauled in. They get disciplined, actually. It's dealing with individual actions.

But think of this as an iceberg, and this is the part that's above water. If that's the piece that's in place, the "law and order response" piece, you're pushing down on this iceberg. It just pops back up. You're not really changing the values that gave rise to the bullying. So there's got to be an educational component, a continuing educational component because it's inevitable that, without it, the bullying will be inevitable, and you're only dealing with individuals.

So, secondly, there's the systemic piece – what policies are in place, what curriculum is in place. The ideas that people have, they learned from the system. Ideas then inform actions.

These pieces are all interrelated, of course. The system shapes individual actions – what they allow to happen and what they don't allow to happen.

Thirdly, actions of people in power shape the system. People learn from how they see people being treated. So we've got this kind of circular system. So there's got to be a political component that deals with the systemic stuff. Those three areas all have to be dealt with, something transformative.

What Students Say about It

Sian

Sian is white, female, and in Grade 11 like Joey. Less deliberate than Joey, she is a bundle of energy, oblivious to all punctuation, except exclamation marks, when she speaks:

> Oh my God! Joey did it! He wanted to come out for Black History Month and the reason – and the reason he wanted to do it is because it's pretty much a heterosexual Christian assembly at this school, and so we wanted to represent black queers. So Joey is like, "I will write a poem," and he wrote a poem talking about all this oppression, how his brothers and sisters are putting him down.
>
> Everyone knows him 'cause he's just a wonderful person. He's extremely involved in the school and everyone's like, "Oh my God!"

When I ask Sian to elaborate on what she means by characterizing the assembly as "Christian" in past years, she is very perceptive in drawing a distinction between homophobia, heterosexism, and heteronormativity:

> No, it's not homophobic, I wouldn't say. It's not really hostile or stupid and based in fear of queers. It's more that they just assume that everybody is the same. It's so important that the humungous heterosexualness of things gets attention, too, and that's what's so cool about Joey's poem. It's about him, but it makes people think about themselves because now they have to ask themselves if they feel any different about Joey now and why that is. It's not just about queers, you know. The straight kids and teachers, too, need to think about their own gender prisons. It's not always because they're homophobic but that sometimes everything is just so heterosexual, and that's damaging, too.

Sian is one of the students at Brookwood who helped to found a gay-straight alliance, which in her school is called Closet Space. Sian tells me, "I don't know if Closet Space helps with dealing with heterosexism – it's so strong at this school – but it's helpful in providing a refuge from it."

Am I Safe Here?

Dalton

When I speak with Dalton, he is in his final year at Brookwood. Dalton is very involved in LGBTQ politics in Toronto and by his own assessment "probably not your typical queer kid in high school" because he has "always read and been politically aware and active." He is finely attuned to the ways that schools exclude LGBTQ students, intentionally or not, which appear understated to many but are keenly felt by every LGBTQ student in the school:

> Take dance posters. The pictures they would use to inform you of the dance. Not only did they tell you where, what day, and what time, but also who. There was always a photograph cut out from some magazine of a male and female, so that heteronormativity sort of skews all the day-to-day things and makes life in schools pretty heterosexist.

Dalton has spoken up in ways other LGBTQ students might not. As he puts it, "I was maybe a bit less afraid of being 'outed' in high school. In fact, I was out, but that was because I had a boyfriend and I didn't want to pretend that I didn't."

Dalton, like all of the LGBTQ students I meet, is quite familiar with the Triangle Program:

> Towards the end of my high school years, after I'd come out to myself and knew a little bit about the community, I would have become much more aware of the Triangle Program. But I always knew that the Triangle Program was there and – well, it's not exactly a utopian place for queer students, but it was a refuge. Some queer students who find themselves in really awful situations, not just heteronormative or heterosexist complaints, but where all of that has just led students to really pick on and bully somebody, so they have to get out. It's a transitional program for students who weren't surviving in other places and needed a bridging element, after which they were supposed to go back into a regular-stream high school. But I never would have considered going into a program like that myself.
>
> Earlier on in my high school, from Grade 9 to 10, it wouldn't have occurred to me that – because I wasn't fully out to myself – it wouldn't have occurred to me that I could belong in a gay-lesbian high school.

But views on them in general? I think the Triangle Program is a really crucial support for students. I wish more school boards had similar programs. I think it's an interesting possibility.

LGBTQ Lives in the Curriculum

In 1999, Peter Corren and Murray Corren, two concerned parents of a gay son, filed a human rights complaint against the Ministry of Education in British Columbia – not just against one particular school district. The basis of the Correns' legal action was that the British Columbia curriculum discriminated against gay, lesbian, bisexual, and transgender students.

Specifically, the Correns complained that the ministry failed to make the provincial curriculum inclusive of positive and accurate portrayals of LGBTQ students and same-sex families. The Correns called this a failure to depict "queer realities." Even though that was years ago, the same charge could be levelled today against many schools.

The Correns settled their litigation with the province in 2006. The Ministry of Education agreed to establish a Grade 12 social justice course reflecting those "queer realities." Unfortunately, the course was optional. An optional course has the advantage of provincial approval. However, the kind of corner-to-corner cultural transformation imagined by Gabe Picard will require obligatory curricular change.

Peter Corren has since died; however, I had the opportunity to speak with the Correns before his death. They spoke to me about the importance of implicating heterosexual students in educative programs on the grounds that they are implicated in the regime of oppression in schools. This was a subject about which they had been thinking for some time.

As much as both stressed the importance of equity policies that call for the presentation of LGBTQ realities in the curriculum, they preferred policies that also encourage heterosexual students to contemplate their own privilege. Murray said,

> When we were, initially, in negotiations with the Ministry of Education to settle the curriculum human rights complaint, the director of

Am I Safe Here?

governance was in attendance at that initial meeting, and he looked at me and said, "I don't really understand what this is all about." And I knew it was a leading question. And so I said to him, "Well, here's a metaphor that I believe works really well to explain why I think this is important. Public education provides both a mirror and a window to students in classrooms. The mirror is there to reflect back to them their realities. So the curriculum reflects students' realities. It also provides a window onto the world about those who are different from you and their realities. So queer kids sitting in a classroom, or children of queer parents sitting in a classroom, have the right to look into that mirror and see their realities reflected back to them. And straight kids sitting in that classroom have the right to that window into a world which up until now has been portrayed as being immoral, objectionable, sick, criminal – and also, at the same time, to be a mirror on their social realities."

So it's a two-way process. And so we're here in this human rights complaint not only to provide an educational environment that is supportive of queer kids and queer families but also to provide those kids who come from heterosexual families, who are themselves heterosexual, to learn about the realities of queer people – but also their own realities in terms of their own sense of masculinity and femininity and that it's cultural – because homophobia and heterosexism comes out of that.

But for the Correns – and Tim McCaskell, Carla at Elizabeth Coyt Alternative School, and most of the students and teachers I spoke to – the principal change they wanted to see was a curriculum that acknowledged but also embraced the content of LGBTQ lives, LGBTQ realities.

Murray Corren stressed that LGBTQ realities "had to" be a part of the curriculum and dialogue, in some form or another, starting in the early grades and continuing throughout the entire time students are in school. He talked about what that might look like at each grade:

It depends on the age level. At an early age level, just simply talking about the whole variety and models of family configurations we have in our society. It's okay to have two moms or two dads. First of all, that they're there and that it's okay. You start with ground rules like that. And then dealing with the name-calling from a very early age. Providing children with a clear rationale as to why it's not appropriate. Teaching children about being socially responsible.

And when they start to move into the intermediate grades, teaching them about the consequences of social injustice in our society. At that age, they are able to understand it and know what the effects of social injustice are. So that by the time kids get to high school, you can begin talking about sexual diversity to the point where, I believe, sexual-health education needs to deal with every kind of sexual diversity and, inevitably, social justice across the curriculum.

Peter Corren agreed, offering this succinct comment about the heteronormative school environment: "What you think is normal is culturally normal, or you've been influenced to think that way. We had to get at that in our settlement."

He also stressed the importance of dealing with the issue of having someone to "look up to":

But you also have to get into the issue of positive role models. The contributions of gay and lesbian people, past and present. You don't have to make a big deal of it. All you do is you have those conversations that there are people from all walks of life who have contributed to science, technology, and art ...

And you've got to look at the differences between urban and rural areas. Kids in rural areas feel very isolated. If they can make that connection to people like themselves, it builds up self-esteem and all sorts of things.

Gay-Straight Alliances

Murray Corren told me why gay-straight alliances (GSAs) are important: "Kids need to know that there are those there, be it teachers or whoever, who are there to support them and provide them with a safe place where they can go just to be themselves."

Am I Safe Here?

"Being yourself" has limits at some schools. Murray told me, "One administrator didn't like the word *queer*. He asked, 'Can we use a different word?' Teachers were tearing down posters."

Tim McCaskell, in his role as a school district equity officer, witnessed the birth of GSAs in Toronto:

> They're happening. We tried to get one set up in a Catholic school, and we got permission to do so. They are difficult. When I was there, what we had was a lesbian-gay kid support group for the whole system, and we got maybe a dozen or so kids that would come to a central area of the school ...
>
> You usually get kids in the upper grades who are finally beginning to come out and whose contact with the ghetto in the outside world has given them a bit of self-confidence, and they will find a teacher that will be the staff adviser and will get one of these things set up.

Diana Goundrey, one of the advisers to Brookwood's GSA, describes the school's treatment of LGBTQ students:

> There are teachers who have taken a really active role in making students feel comfortable. They deal with homophobia and queer issues in class through the curriculum. So that happens. I've had parents come and comment on how they wanted their kid to come here because they saw that little poster. One of my colleagues said that, also. That was one of her – one of the reasons she decided to stay at this school, because she saw the posters and felt immediately comfortable.
>
> And there's our group – there's Closet Space. And everybody in the school has been completely welcoming. When we decided we were gonna do this club, it was just like great, okay, another club to add to the list. We were included in a – I don't know what you call it – like a club fair, let's say, where Grade 9 and 10 kids – where kids can go and look at all the different clubs, and everybody had things set up.
>
> And we were set up there, and it was like we were a club like any other club. I think it was alphabetical, so it wasn't like we were stuck at the corner or something. We make announcements. It's just like any other club. It has been really good.

PLEASE POST
A GAY AND GAY POSITIVE
GROUP OPEN TO
STUDENTS AND STAFF

Closet

Space

ASK YOUR GUIDANCE
COUNSELLOR FOR DETAILS!

Poster for Closet Space, Brookwood Collegiate and Vocational
School's gay-straight alliance

Diana has seen how a GSA can be a powerful force of "resistance in [her] school to the general school climate." Her assessment of the power of the Closet Space posters is far removed from Gabe Picard's lone "Safe Space" sign tucked away in his high school in Thunder Bay. Diana says,

> When I see those Closet Space posters ... I'm amazed. And I'm amazed
> at where I see those in the school. If I go into the metal shop, it's hanging

Am I Safe Here?

there. Or if I go into the auto shop, it's hanging there. It's the first thing you see when you walk in the front door of the school. I know that's maybe a small thing – but it means a lot to kids.

Terrence and Sam

Terrence and Sam, two Asian Canadian gay males, are both seventeen when I meet them. In their last year of high school at Grosvenor Secondary School in Toronto, they decided to establish Grosvenor's first GSA. Terrence and Sam approached Mr. Taylor, a heterosexual teacher in their school, to enlist his support, which was generously extended.

Unfortunately, the "blunt" forces of heterosexism responded with counter-resistance. A number of students used the school newspaper to complain about the GSA. As Terrence tells me, "I think they were trying to rally the troops against us. The usual methods weren't working."

For weeks, a debate raged in the pages of Grosvenor's school paper. The following article, by C.B., was titled "Just Not Right":

> The emergence of the Gay-Straight Alliance at the school has certainly brought a degree of tension and discomfort in the community. Although I truly believe the GSA has been well received and the community has been very respectful, the whole idea and some of the actions taken have made me personally and many others think about their views on homosexuals. I encourage everyone to think long and hard about what is being preached. The introduction of the GSA has definitely made me think long and hard about homosexuals in the [Grosvenor] community and homosexuals in general. Before the presentations I was indifferent about homosexuals and thought they should be treated equally and that they can do whatever they want to do because it will not affect me. However, after thinking hard I have become more opinionated.
>
> Homosexuals should not be discriminated, they should be treated as human beings and should not be made fun of or disadvantaged due to their sexual preference.
>
> Moreover, they should not be discriminated for their (in some cases) eccentric actions around their peers. However, why do people have sexual preference? Gays do not just enjoy the company of other men. The purpose of choosing sexual orientation is to have sexual interactions with one

another. I would like to use the example of gay men to illustrate my point. By no means am I a scientist or know exactly what the functions of the sexual organs are but it is clear the only two sexual organs for reproduction are the penis and the vagina which only when used together produce offspring. I'm not going to get into the specifics on gays, but they have only one sexual alternative, it just does not work, and the possibility of reproduction is scientifically impossible! Whether you believe in a god or not everyone can agree this sexual interaction is not right, the interaction is physically wrong and those who conduct themselves in this manner should definitely not be supported. I don't mean they should be reprimanded or physically or verbally abused. Homosexuals can/should still maintain friendships with straights. They should feel comfortable in our community and accepted but they should know that there [sic] actions biologically are improper and you cannot argue otherwise. Just as straight humans must cope with and accept gays, gays must realize and cope with the fact that their sexual actions are not condoned by society ...

Everyone should look down deep and share what they truly believe, it will be much more constructive than the GSA telling us what the right and wrong ways to act are.

Sometime after the ruckus has died down, Terrence looks back on the episode and sums it up this way:

I've seen this before. People start out by saying, "Well, gay people and lesbians shouldn't be discriminated against, I'm not a bigot," and then they go on to do just that, clinging to their privilege. This was a big thing in our school, as you know. It was very heterosexist. But at the same time, there's no denying there are a lot of kids who want to be cool and not be seen like that. But I have to say, our school is more privileged than a lot of other schools, and things are often more polite here. This was as rude as it got. Which is still bad, but I think at other schools where things are maybe more run by street code, putting up with or even liking the idea of having a GSA wouldn't be seen as an attempt to be cool, it could get pretty bad. I could see lots of kids being afraid to go. Like in a small town or a more rural school. Even here, lots of times it's girls who show up at GSAs because they have a queer friend and they want to go.

Am I Safe Here?

Sam recalls that the letters in the student newspaper went back and forth for weeks. Together, Sam and Terrence penned a first response, titled "Just So Misinformed":

The publishing of C.B.'s article in last week's [newspaper], entitled *Just Not Right*, has certainly brought a multitude of mixed emotions to [our] community. While C.B.'s opinion should be respected, his argument is flawed with misconceptions. Before I share my own view on the issue, I'd like to ask the school community to put things into perspective. Any time there is a reference towards sexual orientation that you have trouble relating to, imagine that reference applying to yourself. Then you will be able to forge your own opinion on the issue at hand, as opposed to being influenced by the argument's face value.

Even before the Gay-Straight Alliance was revived, I knew that there would be misconceptions concerning its role in the school. I was afraid that people would feel that the GSA was trying to force ideas of what's "right" and "wrong" into their heads, to change their opinion. The GSA's mandate was never to tell the school community how to act[,] it was only to provoke self-introspection within the individual and discussion within the school. As a representative of the GSA, I'm hoping to provide an alternate view to the issue, inspiring thought and discussion.

He raises a point worthy of discussion – physiologically and biologically, the penis and vagina do "fit." He is also aware that the reproductive systems, as inherent in the name, are for reproduction. Does that mean sexual intercourse is for the sole purpose of reproduction? Absolutely not. The reality is that few people have sex only for the purpose of reproduction. Most even try to prevent it from happening by using contraceptives. Frankly, the majority of people have sex for pleasure and sexual gratification, not for procreation. Furthermore, some heterosexuals also participate in other sexual acts that do not necessarily involve the interaction between the male and female sexual organs – oral sex, for example. The heterosexist belief that straight, penis-to-vagina sex is the only acceptable way to have intercourse is, in a word, misguided.

Also, according to C.B. he feels that homosexual relationships are purely for sexual reasons. As I mentioned before, let's put things into perspective, through the eyes of a heterosexual. The following is a direct quote from his *Just Not Right*, with words referring to homosexuality reversed and referring to heterosexuals instead: "Straights do not just enjoy the company of the opposite sex. The purpose of choosing an orientation is to have sexual interactions with one another." This statement simply is not true. Heterosexual relationships are not based solely upon sex. Love, a genuine care for another person, exists in heterosexual relationships, and the same applies for homosexuals.

I would also like to address how C.B. seems to believe that sexual orientation is a choice. Sexual orientation is not a conscious decision; people do not consciously decide to be gay or straight – they are who they are, and that cannot be changed. Also, it can be agreed upon that gays have been (and still are) discriminated against in various societies. Given that, who would make the conscious decision to be gay and be discriminated against, living a life of doubt, fear, rejection, and possible loneliness? Homosexuality is also not limited to humans either. There have been many documented cases of homosexual animal behaviour. To cite a specific example, Roy and Silo are two male penguins at the Central Park Zoo in Manhattan. In the past seven years, they have been inseparable, and have been seen to entwine their necks, vocalize to each other, and have sex. When offered female companionship, they refused. They've even raised their own chick, Tango, taking good care of it ever since it was just an egg.

Reading the noted article, it really brought to my attention how misled the community could be. It further strengthens why the Gay-Straight Alliance is here. We are here to inform you with all the information we can and THEN you can devise your own opinion. We merely want everyone to be aware and more informed of a topic that is so quieted in most societies. When putting yourself in the other's shoes, how does it feel to be told that what comes naturally to you is wrong? How does it feel when someone tells you that what you truly believe in is wrong? Is this truly tolerance and acceptance when someone tells you that who you are is wrong?

The student who caused the uproar, C.B., wrote several more letters, not exactly apologetic, but each succeeding response was written with less and less confidence as the letter writer became, in Terrence's words, "kind of isolated in a spotlight." The school's official response was to stand behind Sam and Terrence and the GSA. Sam tells me,

> There's no doubt we had a lot of institutional support, but there's also no doubt that we got a lot of "looks" to let us know what some people thought, and what they thought was that they didn't like the idea of a GSA at this school. So even though C.B. was isolated, there's no doubt that that isolation was official and that even now, things are resuming to the way they were before. Some of the parents complained, too, but the administration told them to take a hike.
>
> So even though Terrence and I knew the school was officially behind us, especially Mr. Taylor, you knew that some people didn't. But I think the important thing is that you knew the official position was "the GSA stays," and that's important not just for Terrence and me but also because you want the up-and-coming students who might be thinking of taking it over some day, maybe next year, to see that. And you especially want the straight hetero kids to see that.

Both Terrence and Sam worry about what will happen to the GSA after they graduate. However, they both express confidence in the commitment of the club's teacher adviser, Mr. Taylor. They believe he will ensure its continued survival. Mr. Taylor confirms to me that his goal is to ensure that the GSA continues after Terrence and Sam graduate.

Over a year after first meeting Terrence and Sam, I run into Sam one night in Toronto. He tells me that he is studying design and that he is overwhelmed but really enjoying university.

I ask him to look back on his experience with the GSA and the debate his actions inspired in the school newspaper. We talk for a few minutes about the "heteronormative citizenship"[3] Terrence and Sam tried to address. He says,

> You know, it's interesting. It seems to me, now, that there was much less homophobia there and much more protection of heteronormative citizenship in response to what we were doing than I wanted to see at the

time, or could see. I wanted, I think, to see this as something that C.B. was doing because he was homophobic. And it's funny because it wasn't homophobia that caused Terrence and me to want to start that group, it was just the general hetero nature of the school. I hadn't really been aware of a lot of homophobia at Grosvenor, it was the hetero culture that we found we had to do something about.

Crossing the Gender Line

Ryan, the fifteen-year-old student at Triangle, lasted less than four months at his original high school before seeking a transfer out.

Ryan is tall, slim, and dressed in baggy pants, a baggy shirt, and a baseball cap worn backward. He has very long hair, particularly at the front, with bangs in his eyes that hang down almost to the middle of his nose. He tells me that his mother thinks he looks like a sheepdog.

Ryan thinks he "looks gay." But seeing him on his skateboard in the street or on the bus with his skateboard under his arm, most people likely see him as a "skater kid" before thinking he is gay. Only later do I notice that Ryan is wearing eye makeup and fingernail polish.

Ryan tells me that he thinks "gender and heteronormativity" are "more important to straight students than bashing queer students." Ryan's perspective interests me because most of the students who have spoken with me are in the higher grades. Most of the lower-year students I've encountered are in mainstream schools, cognizant of the price of not fitting in.

Ryan has already transferred out of such an environment to Triangle. He tells me about the following incident that happened in his Grade 9 English class:

> Bashing queer students is what comes after. It starts with everybody doing the boy thing, the girl thing, the "het" thing. Then to prove that they're normal, they'll look around to bash a couple of queers.
>
> Let me tell you what happened in Grade 9 this year. The English teacher was saying to us, "Okay, you have two choices of which book you can read." I can't even remember what they were. And she said, "The girls

Am I Safe Here?

will want to read this one, and the boys would want to read this other one. Okay," she says, "which book do you want?"

And then she went through the entire class list, calling out everybody's name one by one, and I remember thinking, okay, so now we've got all this gender pressure on us to choose the books she's laid out for us by this boy-girl rule and there's – I remember thinking, you know, I really feel this pressure now to choose the boy book. I really resented that she did that, and I resented even more that we all succumbed to what she basically set out for us to do. Now why do we all know to do that? And why did we do it? There wasn't one person, male or female, including me, who didn't. Not one.

Ryan describes what finally drove him to transfer to Triangle:

I really couldn't take it there anymore. It was really hard not only to be out, with all the pressure to conform to the straight structure, but you kind of get harassed in the hallways. You'd have people yelling at you, and you just wanted to be left alone. And I had kind of gotten – I'm not sure if it was mugged, but on my way to school for some reason, this guy started throwing snowballs at me and I ignored him. And then after I kept ignoring it, he crossed the street and then decided to smash me into a fence and start shoving snow down my clothes. And, well, there was a suicide type thing and I had to go to the hospital. I'd been thinking about it before I came to Triangle. I didn't really feel like staying at my school after that. It was really hard not only to be out, but you kind of get harassed in the hallways. I had people yelling at me and coming up to me and asking, "Yo, guy, why are you so gay?" And I just wanted to be left alone. So I just tried to get away as fast as I could.

Ryan adds something very interesting: "I think most of it was more homophobia and the gender-binary system because everybody had an extreme problem with the nail polish or the eyeliner. I had some friends who had no problem accepting that I was gay but would make comments about the fingernail polish and eyeliner."

These sorts of gender expectations also led James, another student at Triangle, a year older than Ryan, to leave his original high school:

I found the expectations of sexuality and gender to be more of a problem personally than bullying. My sexuality I could hide. That is not a good thing and I am not saying it's a good thing and I would be unhappy if someone took what I am saying to support that. But hiding kept you a safe distance from being bullied. But the *expectations* of gender and being straight, I couldn't escape and couldn't hide from that. Just being a boy brought you into contact with their power. If you were a girl, it brought you into contact with their power and it defined you. What do you do with that for four years?

Ryan emphasizes that he thinks crossing the gender line of what is appropriate for boys is of more importance and greater significance in the minds of some high school students. Why does Ryan think his friends felt the need to comment? "To make themselves feel more secure," he says. Then he waves and takes off down the street on his skateboard.

Gendered Spaces

Diana Goundrey is excited about the Closet Space posters hanging in the metal shop and the machine shop at Brookwood. Many LGBTQ students raise the issue of school space as gendered space or school space as heteronormative space. To these students, some school spaces can be read as threatening, and some school spaces can be read as safer, depending upon the degree to which the space is "masculine" or "heteronormative" or "heterosexist."

Strikingly, all the students I speak to point to machine shops, woodworking shops, and metal shops as some of the most threatening spaces in schools – second only to school gyms and physical-education classes. But Diana Goundrey tells me,

> The most supportive people have been the tech guys. I'll go downstairs and I'll call the auto guys and say listen, I need a float for the Pride Parade. They'll joke. They'll say, "I don't know if I can find any gay tow trucks. I'll see." But they'll do it. They'll make jokes or whatever. But they'll do it.
>
> I think things have just changed, and they've realized, because some of them have been victims. They've had – and they see kids get picked on because they're not macho enough. So they're pretty cool about that.

Kyle, a Grade 12 student at Brookwood, offers a different take on Goundrey's observation: "That's because she's a woman. The tech guys, the phys ed teachers, they treat females differently. They're happy to do her a favour because she's pretty. What do they say when she leaves, I'd like to know? That little poster provides cover."

When I ask Kyle whether there are any spaces at his school that are more physically threatening or safer than other spaces, or more gendered, he confirms that there are. But he points out that school space is sometimes gendered in unexpected, even contradictory, ways:

Yes, I definitely read space like that. Sometimes, I was wrong. A space where I was wrong was in the art house. It's a slightly separate building, a separate entity in the building. It's perceived to be the only place in the school that represents school identity in a positive way. But there was a course taught in there by a real straight guy, and it was a junior course, but it didn't engage me. The art house wasn't really a gay space once I investigated it, even though on the surface people probably thought it was. And the students wanted it to be.

On the other hand, drama was only because of the teacher. Not the students. There the students were real closety, whether because they didn't want to get typecast or what, I don't know. So you had to watch out because of the students. Then there was that art space. I wouldn't say that the art space, in general, was queer space because of the students who made it up. It wasn't very comfortable, again, because of the students. So these spaces were both perceived one way, positively, I think, because of art and drama, but occupying those spaces was different.

I avoided spaces where I didn't want to be, areas where there were young students, where these hetero issues seemed more immediate, and sort of the students who were the least academic. Students doing very masculine things like shop or woodwork, which to me was more threatening.

Heterosexist Geography

Len, the Grade 12 student at Trimble Collegiate Institute who earlier labelled the hallways of his school as heterosexist, talks to me more about the "rule" or "regulation" of space by his school's heteronormative citizens:

Like I said, I avoided hallways because they were ruled by this dominating culture in this school. There were certain areas of the school and certain people that I instinctively avoided, because they were very dominating, even by how they looked at you – there was a dominating culture in my school and they were it and they let you know. And the cool, straight kids would hang out and sort of patrol their space, and so walking through that hallway was always a little bit uncomfortable for me. They didn't even say anything. They were there and they looked at you and let you know you weren't part of their heterosexist geography because you were queer.

Len considers whether "straight" students have power that he does not and, if so, what the source of that power is and how it is exercised. He speaks to me about how LGBTQ students experience marginalization as a result of spatial practices:

I think it was more of a situation in which they had social power. They had a certain prestige within the school, and that comes about through, among other things, normative gender and sexual presentation. I think the students who are perceived as cool feel the need to maintain that status. And the way they interacted with each other was also part of this – whether that power came from displaying signs of affection in the hallways or talking about the other gender in certain kinds of sexualized ways.

That personal gender presentation was really normative, so the guys all looked and dressed a certain way. They all had this swagger and would wear baseball caps, pants a certain way, and talk in a certain way to their friends. A lot of hashing around and things like calling their friends by their last names – a certain way of talking, dressing, of moving.

The women – I would say the same thing. All sorts of normative, very feminine presentation. They exuded their sexuality. It was a very dominant kind of sexuality. I think being heteronormative and sexist and even homophobic was part and parcel of it. And it goes on without most of them consciously thinking about it.

Len is quick to point out that this kind of authority has never been exercised against him personally:

Am I Safe Here?

It hasn't been. But I am not sure that anyone *would*. I have a kind of citizenship in the school. No one has ever called me a fag, ever. Nobody ever called me queer, and I actually did date a few girls. And I am a very popular student, well known throughout the school. I am, you know, involved. So, you see, I have a significant role in the school culture that afford[ed] me a visibility even when I wasn't out, even though I didn't identify myself as gay the way some students do.

Len also seems older than he is. He attributes this to the fact that he is involved in a relationship. Len believes his boyfriend gave him a strength against those who might have moved against him: "Once I started showing up with my boyfriend, well ... But I still don't think anyone would have dared cross me just because of who I am in the school. It's too late to get me. I'm established. So I don't feel I've paid that price. However, that doesn't mean I don't feel something."

Unlike at Sylvia Avenue and Burton School, there are no courses dealing with gender and culture at Trimble Collegiate, where Len goes to school. Nonetheless, Len has read widely on his own. He is perceptive and generous enough to distinguish between his personal experiences and his position in the broader cultural landscape of his school:

When you're queer, you're differentiated the minute you walk down the hallway or enter the classroom. You can't relate and they don't let you relate. In the halls, it's the students; in the classrooms, it includes the teacher and the curriculum. The upside to that, I think, is an awareness of how the school and the world works, which gives you a target, allows you to know what to change. Now, can most queer kids do that when they're fourteen years old?

When you're fourteen years old, it can be crippling, but you're very aware that all of these trappings are just that. They're trappings. That's why it's important that there are students in upper grades, like me, like others, and teachers, who can maybe speak out or just make themselves known by being out, just through their presence, to change things, maybe, but also for those fourteen-year-old students in Grade 9.

But school, for me, is still a very oppressive experience because of the expectations of gender and sexuality. I think for queer students, there's a real tie, a real relationship, between being gay or lesbian and gender – sexuality and gender. In fact, the most oppressive part of high school for me is the expectations placed on me because I was a boy, these straight kids I was talking about, this whole straight culture. I just find that so restricting and more than just restricting, I feel it as a weight. A weight that I felt was going to crush me, maybe until I met my boyfriend – and brought him to school.

Even though Len is aware of his secure social position within the school, he makes it clear that he has witnessed incidents of physical and verbal bullying. He explains to me how such incidents were handled:

Security was the frontman. They would physically stop it, catch it, and then take the offender to the VPs, whose full-time job it was to mete out student discipline. Our VPs are one black male, two white females. They respond in the typical fashion, following the rubric of what they needed to do. In other words, get rid of the offender. Once students were suspended ... well, they were gone.

Suspending students, I would say, is not entirely effective because it was treating the problem too close towards the end of the spectrum, ignoring the start and focusing on the end of a problem. That's too close to the end, but it's what most schools do to show they're doing anything. That's my main criticism. There are not enough resources, money and otherwise, put into dealing with all of the systemic problems.

Len reflects on whether it is possible to improve the experiences of LGBTQ students in schools. Is there anything the school can do officially? He says,

In terms of what the VPs think is their "official" role, I think they spend a lot of their minute-to-minute energy dealing with, "Look at what you did, this bad thing, this is what's going to happen to you now," instead of saying, "This is what's happening in the school, this is a huge problem, let's look at our equity obligations." It doesn't fit into their day. Look at how the system of education is putting all these people in the same classroom and then not doing anything to educate them about each other. Even though we have this mighty equity policy.

Len is another student who supports policies that stress equity, not just punitive responses to incidents of bullying. Like so many others, he champions an equitable and inclusive approach. He sees this as the best means to bring about the kind of day-to-day experience he would like to see LGBTQ students have in school:

Yes, I do think these policies could improve schools the way I'd like to see them improved. Unless I'm wrong, I think ... equity ... talks a lot about school climate or environment or something like that. And that's what is the big thing for me. The general climate. But general climate means you have to think about "the general climate" and that means thinking about straight kids, too. They're the ones most responsible for the climate.

I think that my experiences are the result of how straight kids think and act about themselves ... I don't want to generalize, but I think that gay people are automatically more attuned to the demands of gender, the demands of heterosexuality, than straight kids are. So somehow you have to get at that straight culture, at how straight kids thrash around and present themselves. I mean if somebody hits somebody or even calls you a fag or a dyke, that's not allowed. And everybody knows it's not allowed. So they've got that covered. The climate stuff, not so much. How straight kids present themselves, not so much.

But to me those are two different things: first there's the culture and second there's the homophobia. And so, somehow, the policies have to get at both of those things, and I think they do, with the homophobia, or the emphasis being on school safety, or they're trying. I don't think the schools even think about the other part. And they should. Change the way gender plays out in sports, in phys ed, in the shops, in the masculinized spaces of the school, the homophobic teachers. Start studying gender and presentation of gender in the curriculum. That's what I'd do. That's where I'd start. The policies are saying what's needed to be said, but they have to lead to changes in the curriculum, changes in the hallways. Why does the school dance poster have a picture of a boy and girl on it?

I am not surprised to hear, again, somebody bring up the subject of school dances. School dances and the images used in posters to promote them have been talked about many times. I am reminded of the "culture jamming" exercise in Sharon Dominick's classroom and of her walls covered in images from current magazines.

In conclusion, Len offers me his definition of bullying. Not surprisingly, it is broad: "I'll tell you what I would consider bullying against me. If someone inhibited me from doing something I wanted to do, or if someone inhibited me from being who I wanted to be ... so if someone was an obstacle for me, I would consider that bullying."

Teachers and Administrators: Part of the Problem

At an anti-bullying conference I attend in Toronto, I speak with Michael, a Grade 12 student, who tells me, "I mean my teacher is up there gay bashing. Why wouldn't I want to stay in the closet where it's safe?"

Noel is a very large, strong-looking eighteen-year-old male student at Triangle. He makes an interesting point about the irony of equity policies, noting that the very targets of equity – the privilege and prestige enjoyed by some – are precisely the characteristics that those imbued with advantage do not wish to give up:

> When I was at that school, I did a parenting course and they were talking about marriage. Do your ideal marriage. And I put a guy. And the teacher, she would refuse to mark it. The teacher refused to mark it. And she even went to the principal. And then I was getting mocked by the teacher and the principal ... Where me and my friends ate lunch was right in front of the principal's offices in the hall. They knew what they were doing. Somebody would see me standing there outside the principal's office and yell, "What did you do now, gay boy?" And then when the principal, when she called me in, she heard them, so she said, "See, your attitude,

because you're out, you provoke those kind of remarks." And that's what she said to me.

And she knows my history about my dad, about how my dad died when I was twelve years old. So she made a comment that sticks to me to this day: "It's because of your dad, he didn't get to teach you certain stuff." And I'm like, "I'm gay 'cause my dad ...?"

I think it bugged them that I didn't fit a stereotype. I mean, to me, I'm the worst fashion guy and I don't pretend to have good fashion. It's like this T-shirt and a sweater. And I don't know anything about it. Plus my school was such a heterosexist place. You're not gay because you're not fashionable, you don't talk gay, you're not feminine, you're not everything the stereotypical gay guy is. So that made them uncomfortable to think that they couldn't tell who was gay and who wasn't. Students and teachers, they weren't interested in equity because equity is a direct threat to their status in the school.

Lorna Gillespie at Trimble Collegiate makes a similar point, referring to what she calls the "inherent conservativism" of teachers. "They are a conservative bunch," she tells me over lunch. When I ask whether her characterization is overly broad, she thinks for a moment and then explains,

Teachers tend to be white, they tend to be middle-class, they tend to come from families that are relatively privileged, and so they've gone to university, they've done the humanities thing, and they don't know what to do, so they decided to be a teacher. That's a general statement, for sure. And what do whites do with their power? Not much. Because they're conservative and equity is a threat to them. And the students sometimes are just as conservative and just as desperate to hold onto their big-man or big-chick status.

So I think there's a number of things. One, they just don't see it as part of their job. Two, they're conservative or homophobic. A third reason is that they may just be ignorant. I think most of them don't even think about doing it. It's not like they think, "Oh I would like to do this but I'm scared." And, fourth, they're afraid if they do make a bid towards equity, they won't have the support of their fellow teachers because we know how conservative teachers are and maybe unlikely to offer the kind of support that's needed to encourage other teachers to step up. And last, if they are aware of equity, it's a threat to their own privilege. And I think some of them want the status quo to continue in their students – in some of their students.

Go Directly to the VP's Office

At the anti-bullying conference in Toronto, I speak with a vice-principal who blames a good deal of the lack of implementation of the equity policies on vice-principals:

> It's political. The vice-principal's office is a political office. Nobody who's in there – I shouldn't say nobody, but I will – wants to stay in there. They have an eye on a higher office. Nobody wants trouble. Nobody wants to rock the boat. Implementing equity rocks the boat and draws unwanted attention to your school. That's not the way to get ahead.

At the same conference, I ask a guidance counsellor for his take on the political nature of the vice-principal's office:

> There are some very good policies ... but sometimes they don't get carried out at a particular school because they're given to the VP to deal with, and then the VP has political aspirations, and wants to go further ahead in his or her career, and doesn't want to have anything controversial going on, and that is an impediment to a particular school's being transformed to a more progressive place.

When I relay these opinions to Diana Goundrey, the guidance counsellor at Brookwood, she says, "I think I would agree. But I don't think people actively sabotage the equity policies. I think what happens is they don't have time. They don't see it as a priority. They see safe schools as a bigger priority, and they don't see that equity is a part of safety, that it is just as important, because if you've got equity, then you've got safe schools. So sometimes it's that. It's just lack of priority. And sometimes, it's just lack of time."

Am I Safe Here?

A Lack of Resources

A complaint I hear from Jeffrey White, the head of the Triangle Program, is that there is a lack of resources for the implementation of equity policy; he says the school board "needed to put its money where its mouth was." When I first spoke with Jeffrey, he had only recently taken over running the program. Since then, he has dealt with hundreds of students who have arrived at Triangle seeking a safe haven and searching for the equity that does not exist at the schools from which they have fled. Jeffrey tells me,

> The [district] has this wonderful equity policy that's written down, there it is, but who's implementing it? Very few people. There's no money behind implementation of the policy, so all of the principals are aware of it, but it can just sit up on a shelf because there's no money. So equity's not getting done.
>
> Students come to Triangle and start learning about queer realities. One student heard about the equity policy and said, "What? If I knew this was in place, I would've gotten my parents behind me and we would've done more at the school to really have the school do something." And, of course, I'm aware of Gabe Picard's case ... where a school has been taken to court to demand it. Here, we have resources because it's our mandate.

Len at Trimble Collegiate makes a similar observation, citing the lack of resources as part of the difficulty of "giving teeth to equity." I show Len's teacher Lorna several publications I have accumulated in my travels through schools, all proclaiming how to promote equity and safe spaces for LGBTQ students. When I ask her where they came from, she laughs. "These look like those wonderful publications from the equity office that we never see because they land in the vice-principal's office and get buried. Nobody has any time or money to implement any of that stuff."

Starting Early – And Starting with Teachers

Lorna is not convinced that equity would be accomplished even if these publications went to the guidance counsellor, or to the school library, or to the teachers themselves instead of to the vice-principal. In her experience, the first obstacle to successfully teaching about gender and sexuality is convincing teachers that equity is part of their job:

Teachers don't see equity as part of their job. So the number-one reason equity doesn't get addressed is simply that they would say it doesn't relate to their subject. They truly believe that those concerns are just not part of what they've been hired to do. That's an excuse. I think it's relevant to any subject. In fact, [our] *Equity Statement* says that.

Lorna takes a broad view of curriculum reform, convinced that the reforms need to begin in the early grades but also need to be a mandated part of the curriculum:

Well, we definitely have to start early. And it needs to be part of the mandated curriculum. Because otherwise, teachers aren't going to do that. I mean, there are very few elementary teachers who are going right out and dealing with this topic, even if they might want to, because they would be concerned about parents. They definitely would be concerned because so many people think that you don't talk about these things until a certain age, right?

She believes that equity and inclusive education start with teachers:

Well, I think we need to do workshops for teachers first, and I'm going to try to push for this next year. I think we need workshops for the teachers – for teachers, for staff, and for students. We actually had one once where somebody came in to talk to the teachers, just the teachers, about what school was like for queer students, and the teachers at the back of the room turned their chairs around with their back to the people who were presenting and read the paper and ignored them.

Lorna was outraged at the behaviour of her colleagues. She saw their actions as a conscious political statement. She says, "Well, it had to be. You have a guest speaker, you don't turn your back to them." Lorna identifies teacher homophobia or at least lack of comfort with LGBTQ issues as another reason why equity is not undertaken in schools.

Lorna is not the first person to point out that teachers are sometimes homophobic. There is not one student I meet who does not experience homophobia from at least one teacher. There is not one teacher I

Note written by a student and passed to Azmi Jubran during shop class, Handsworth Secondary School, North Vancouver

meet who does not find himself or herself surrounded by homophobic colleagues.

For example, in a case before a human rights tribunal in 2005 (see Chapter 4 for more details), the principal at Azmi Jubran's school testified that he had never seen physical and verbal harassment of the kind to which Azmi had been subjected. Yet Azmi tells me that a good deal of the bullying that he experienced occurred in front of his teachers and sometimes with a teacher's approval or what could be read as approval because of the lack of a heartfelt response to it:

> Many things happened in front of the teacher. Apart from physical and verbal stuff, there were notes being passed around about me.
>
> I specifically remember one. A student wrote a – not wrote, drew – a picture of me and another male holding hands, saying, "Oh isn't this great under the sunlight?" or "Isn't this romantic?" and passed it to me. The teacher saw it, and basically all the teacher did was say, "Whatever you're doing, stop it," and went on with the calculation on the board. He didn't care.

Inclusive Education: A Big Hoopla

When we consider an equity policy that specifically calls for inclusiveness in the school curriculum and environment, concerns about parental and community reaction are ever present. As Lorna tells me,

> Most schools want to avoid it. Like in my class, every year, there's a big hoopla when we discuss homophobia, homosexuality, queer theory, the whole bit. Other teachers wouldn't touch that with a ten-foot pole. They're scared that the parents will say something, and in thirteen years I've had one parent say something. They just don't have a political commitment. They don't see their job as political. They think it's the dissemination of information and that's what you are as a teacher. They don't really understand what I consider to be a teacher to be their idea of a teacher.

I ask Lorna whether the administration, which might have more knowledge of the equity policy than many of the teachers, has ever stepped in and encouraged the teachers to pursue equity concerns in their classrooms. "I have yet to see it," she says. When I ask whether there are any other reasons the administration does not take a proactive role, she explains,

> Well, they're former teachers. And they're former teachers who want to become bureaucrats, so now you're going even more conservative than maybe the other teachers. If you're a teacher and you want to move to be a VP, you're not dedicated to the teaching part in my view. You want to make more money; you want to have more power. And you certainly do not want to rock the boat.
>
> If you're a VP, you're headed for principal. Once you make principal, you might want to go further to be a superintendent, but I have to say I don't think that's necessarily always true, but sometimes.

Referring again to those publications and resources that do exist, the ones intended for teachers to use in order to create equitable and inclusive schools, Lorna describes what happens when those resources that are available arrive in the school:

Let me put it this way. If the school board plunks a new program or idea in the school and says, "Here, this is what you should do to be proactive about gay and lesbian and trans issues," what's going to happen? Well, either nothing is going to happen or teachers like me are going to pick it up and push.

If it was just handed to the admin, zip for the most part, although we do have a VP right now who just went with me to that forum down at the St. Lawrence Centre [for the Arts] on gender identity and sexual orientation that I told you about. She's definitely on board, but I don't think she has the guts to actually do anything right out.

I'll let you know.

A teacher for over twenty years, Lorna speaks from experience: "These kids are so much more conservative than I am. I was born in 1953, but sometimes they act like *they* were born in 1953. I say, 'I'm over fifty years old and I'm so much more with it and radical than you are. What's wrong with you?' But times have changed – I'm a '60s girl."

The Succinct Last Word

When I speak with Jerry, it has been two years since he graduated from Brookwood. He is now very involved with a volunteer group that goes into high schools to educate students about LGBTQ rights. He is also an editor of a local LGBTQ newspaper. Maybe for these reasons, he is very succinct in summing up the difference between the official and un-official ways students learn.

Jerry says to me, "The education part, maybe you'll remember, prob-ably you won't. The *schooling* part, you never forget. Students take that with them for the rest of their lives. Schooling normalizes heterosexism and lets homophobia take root for some."

Summing Up

Pursuing equity in schools depends not only on the extent to which policies are implemented in schools and how they are implemented but also on how they are affected by other cultural factors and social structures at play in schools.

There are insufficient resources and inadequate training and support, at all levels, for educators to create safe, equitable, and inclusive schools. This is seen in many aspects of school life:

- Funding from school districts and school boards is inadequate to implement widespread cultural change.
- Teachers do not receive sufficient training in inclusive education throughout their teacher training and education. As a result, teachers do not see ensuring equity and social justice as part of their job – they see their job as disseminating information, not changing culture.
- Teachers feel they lack sufficient resources to implement equity and inclusion in their classrooms. They also fear a lack of support from other teachers, which is often related to homophobia among school faculty and staff.
- Resources that do exist are often not made available and distributed to teachers. They often go no farther than the vice-principal's office because (1) administrators do not wish to be seen as courting controversy, equity being perceived as controversial; (2) administrators tend to be conservative and to favour the status quo rather than effecting change; or (3) the teachers who become administrators are often those teachers who are less interested in the *teaching* part of what schools do.
- There are few or no "out" teachers or supportive teachers to act as models for LGBTQ youth. This has the correlative effect of discouraging students from taking an active role in changing school culture, leading to further exclusion, not to student connectedness and inclusion.

Safe, equitable, and inclusive schools are more likely to become a reality when the following dynamics are also present:

- Gay-straight alliances are permitted and supported in schools.
- The official curriculum includes and celebrates LGBTQ realities and lives and does so in most subjects. This is particularly needed to counter the negative stereotyping and homophobic construction of LGBTQ persons that goes on in the unofficial spaces of schools every day.
- Students play a role in school governance and disciplinary matters.
- The realities and experiences of LGBTQ persons are reflected not only in the curriculum but also in school activities like drama and art.
- Heterosexual student privilege is implicated in curriculum dealing with the social construction of gender and sexuality.
- LGBTQ teachers are "out" and able to provide role models for students.

When policies and legislation are aimed at responding to isolated incidents of victimization, schools are more likely to follow policies to the letter and more likely to neglect practices that will lead to doing equity and promoting inclusive education. However, in terms of addressing a broader conception of what it means for LGBTQ students to go to school, an approach that focuses on an incident-based response is not effective since the larger school culture is not subject to change.

What Needs to Be Done

- Education and curriculum are key to transforming the homophobic and heteronormative culture of schools.

  - The official curriculum of schools must work to offer positive, celebratory depictions of LGBTQ realities in order to counter the negative stereotyping and homophobic depictions occurring in unofficial school spaces at all grades.
  - Equitable and inclusive education must begin in the early grades and in all courses.

- Those in charge of the governance of schools and school safety must stop seeing bullying, harassment, and aggressive heternormativity as symptoms of "boys being boys" or "girls being girls" and come to understand that there are long-term negative consequences for LGBTQ students who are excluded from a school culture that either does not recognize them or just ignores them, as well as for those who are targeted and victimized by this culture through bullying and other forms of harassment.
- Schools should establish gay-straight alliances; these organizations provide a safe and inclusive space within schools for LGBTQ students, but they also send a message to heterosexual students by acknowledging the presence and value of LGBTQ students. It is important that administrations support GSAs, not fear them as indicators of a school with problems. GSAs and other similar student groups have been shown to be an important component of school reformation.
- The administration must meaningfully support safe, equitable, and inclusive education and policies so that teachers engaging in safe and inclusive practices feel supported and safe.
- Teachers must receive education, training, and workshops on inclusive education practices at all stages of their education and careers.
- Resources and materials to implement these changes must be available so that teachers feel supported with information, training, and resources.
- The work of making schools safe, equitable, and inclusive for LGBTQ students must go on every day – and it has to be mandatory, not optional. It cannot be accomplished with once-a-year sensitivity training or by being included in a social studies unit. Such tokens are not the kind of authentic, inclusive responses needed to achieve the kind of reformation that is required. We must always bear in mind what Katie says at the start of this book: "It's a greater complexity, you know?"

4

Rules to Live By, or
How to Succeed in School without
Really Changing Anything

Rule 1: Snitches get stitches ... So you don't rat.

> – *Diana Goundrey, guidance counsellor*

Rule 2: It's against God to be gay.

> – *Noel, Grade 12 student*

Rule 3: If I call you a fag, then that means I'm not one.

> – *Trista, Grade 11 transgender student*

Rule 1: Don't Rat

Obie Trice's CD *Second Round's on Me* contains a song entitled "Snitch," in which other rappers are featured.[1] The lyrics leave no doubt about norms against snitching and the low social position of anyone who "tells" on someone else:

> Just don't, whatever you do, snitch
> 'Cause you will get hit
> Pray I don't face you, yeah.

The words describe the "street justice" handed out to snitches, revenge that may be exacted against them. Those who snitch to the authorities are perceived as "weak" and buckling under to the law "when the heat's on 'em," leaving no doubt that they have betrayed the group, having gone from "cats" to "rats" in need of "decon."

The music video of the song depicts Trice, Eminem, Akon, and their gang committing a bank robbery. One of them, Rick Gonzalez, captured by the police, snitches, and the entire group is rounded up and sent to jail. At some point, after this group is released, Trice, Eminem, Akon, and the others hound the snitch, and the video ends with the Trice-led group finding Gonzalez and pulling a gun on him. Singing a refrain of the chorus, they shout at him, "You rat bastard!" The music video of the song was edited when it was shown on BET and MTV. On MTV even the title of the track was changed, from "Snitch" to "Mindstate of a Mobster," and the word "snitch" was deleted from the track.

At Sylvia Avenue Collegiate and Vocational School, media teacher Sharon Dominick spends a good deal of time analyzing the hateful and homophobic lyrics of singers, particularly singers like Eminem and other rappers. She tries hard to get her students to consider the power of some rap music. She asks them to consider the damage behind its lyrical assault on LGBTQ students.

Diana Goundrey, guidance counsellor at Brookwood Collegiate and Vocational School, undertakes the same efforts with students and teachers alike. Both Sharon and Diana are familiar with the "anti-rat" or "anti-snitch" culture at both of their schools.

Diana has a list of complaints about the music that students carry around with them. Foremost among her grievances is that hip hop music, in particular, dehumanizes women and LGBTQ people. The lyrics depict how acts of violence against them play out in a culture that relegates would-be rescuers to the outside social position of being a snitch. Safety at Brookwood is security-oriented, implemented by surveillance cameras, two patrolling security guards, and strict enforcement of the zero-tolerance policies against physical harassment. Diana sees "pockets" of equity being pursued on behalf of LGBTQ students at her school but sighs deeply at the obstacles in her way.

She credits a growing number of teachers at her school for supporting equity and promoting anti-bullying programs in the school. However, she is most frustrated by the anti-snitch culture that pervades her school:

Yeah, it's pretty bad. Snitches get stitches. It's a huge problem. There's so much of this gangster, this jail thing, right? We hear a lot of jail talk in a regular school in a way that you never used to hear. I notice it because I used to work with young offenders. So I know – I've seen that happen over the years. And this snitching, this rat thing, that's a real jail thing. So you don't rat. There's that brotherhood amongst thieves, and all that kind of stuff. It's bad. Bad and huge.

I wonder whether Diana means "brotherhood" literally, but she shakes her head, firmly, even as I begin to ask. "No," she says, "it's both boys and girls. It's both."

She is concerned that bullied students have no one to turn to. She sees the anti-snitch culture contributing to a wall of isolation, leaving bullied students to feel that no one will help. She knows how it plays out:

At the beginning of the year ... I thought ... oh ... it's so sad. I thought we had more kids than usual who simply stopped attending in Grade 9, mainly boys. And there seemed to be no reason. It's not like they had poor attendance before that. There seemed to be no reason. They would just stop coming. And they would never give an answer as to why. I tried ... but suspected that they were being bullied, and they just didn't say anything. Wouldn't. Couldn't. They just didn't want to come to school, and they just waited for the next semester, so they could leave. That's what I think. I have nothing to back that up. But it's just strange that these perfectly nice kids, and they were quiet and nice kids. And they just stopped coming. And I wonder if that's what it was. God, I could cry.

Carla and Emma, the two girls at Elizabeth Coyt Alternative School, and Lazy Daisy, who made the art print for me at Burton School, confirm that the anti-snitch culture is no different for girls. All agree that both boys and girls are governed by the anti-snitch code of youth culture. Lazy Daisy says, "At my previous school, stuff would happen to me, but I never said anything because I didn't want to seem like a snake. And I didn't want to draw attention to myself about me being gay. Snake and snitch. Yeah, it's like someone who tells on everybody else. Plus, I'm gay? No thanks."

They're Going to Get Killed

Even though Diana Goundrey is known throughout the school as an ally and a supporter of all students, including LGBTQ students, she knows students will not speak up if they see someone being bullied:

> It's so huge ... So big. Because if they said something, somehow it would get out. Even if you say to a kid, "Look, no one's going to know that you told me this. I'm going to say blah, blah, blah." Even *that* makes them nervous, because if it ever *gets* out, they're going to get killed ... They're going to get killed. And they know that. We can't protect them. Doesn't matter what the school says. Doesn't matter.
>
> Can we stop?

Diana is overwhelmed by what she has been compelled to think about and wants to stop for the day.

Len, the confident Grade 12 student at Trimble Collegiate Institute, confirms how the anti-snitch laws among students discourage speaking up:

> A lot of students don't rat or snitch out of fear. They don't wanna be hurt by the people who are committing these crimes or whatnot. And those people are often in gangs. I would say it's *really* big among black students, particularly Jamaicans.
>
> Just fear. That anti-snitch mentality feeds the fear. There is a definite gang presence at this school. But there are students here who wouldn't be affected by the fear of a gang presence, and they would speak up. I'm one of them. I'd just go to the office, the VP.

Avoid the VP's Office

Noel attended school in a rural area before transferring to the all-LGBTQ Triangle Program. He is earning a few credits to get his Grade 12 diploma. Noel talks about why the vice-principal's office is not a place to report bullying:

> No, I wouldn't do that. Not at my old school, I mean. Maybe in Toronto, you could count on some back-up, but at so many of these other schools, like at my school in North Bay, forget it. You can report it, but nothing's

Am I Safe Here?

going to be done about it. They just don't care. That kind of behaviour, bullying, harassment, it's expected. It's boys being boys. And it's not addressed. I don't know what their deal is, but probably because they're the older generation type of teachers. Where it's like they just don't care. And then there you are, the rat. Whether you're the gay kid or the kid who saw it, if you reported it, you're the rat.

As Noel puts it, there are two groups of people who share the bottom rung: "snitches and fags." "If you're gay and you ask for help, guess what? You're both a fag and a snitch."

Trista, a Grade 11 transgender student at Triangle, agrees: "Yup, a fag and a snitch. Lowest."

Unofficial Law

In the context of the anti-snitch culture, the messages LGBTQ students receive are mixed. Policies confirm equality and inclusiveness, but as Diana points out, "The street says something else: put up with it, don't complain – if you do complain, you're a snitch."

Emma expands on why the anti-snitch code does not dictate how self-governance plays out at Coyt, the social justice school:

Oh, no, there's no anti-snitch codes here. It's very much a school in which the institutional theme of social justice commands something *else*, that we look after each other – especially seniors looking after juniors. We all look out for each other, so if there was an instance where someone's feelings got fairly badly hurt and they recruited a few seniors to go talk to this person, there would be no retribution for that. None. We'd say to that kid, "You're being insensitive and you should probably go apologize." We look after each other. That person would go apologize, and believe me, they would never enforce an anti-snitch code because the social justice theme is so engrained here, they'd know they did something wrong – and now it had been dealt with and it was over.

As always, the students at Burton School and Coyt impress me with their ability to articulate ideas that reinforce the need for a cultural reformation at most other schools that will shift the emphasis to inclusive education and equity. Carla says,

> Yeah. I know what you mean by a code of silence. No, not really, not here. It's really interesting, though. There's sort of an interesting dynamic in our grade because we're larger. There's the people who do sports and then the rest of us, which is really interesting. It's not that we clash, but we just don't really interact much. Our classes are often structured half and half, but we just don't interact much 'cause we can't find much common ground. So, on the other side, among the people who play sports, who are on teams, I've seen that sometimes, the other group of students in our grade, just a little bit of loyalty to the team and don't turn on us, but I haven't found that within our group of friends. And, still, it's not much with the sports half, nothing that would interfere with anybody feeling that bad behaviour wasn't going to be or shouldn't be reported.
>
> But you can see how it might take root among people who felt they were, I don't know, part of a group, somehow, if that feeling were greater than the sense of equity or social justice we pursue here. But thankfully, here, the general culture of equity wins out over any code of silence.

Rule 2: It's against God to Be Gay

When I spoke with Peter Corren in Vancouver about his human rights complaint, he identified "religion" and "religious backlash" from parents as "the foundation of nearly all of the opposition that we've experienced over the ten years of doing anti-homophobic work."

He spoke about the death of Hamed Nastoh, a young man who jumped off a bridge in Vancouver. In particular, he referred to the reaction to Hamed's suicide as an example of the obstacles religion and "religious influence" present to the cultural reformation of schools:

> Hamed Nastoh jumped off the Pattullo Bridge, killed himself, because of bullying, in fact, homophobic bullying, and ... the [British Columbia] Ministry of Education ... decided to take on, to implement, some kind of initiative around bullying in schools.

Am I Safe Here?

And so ... the taskforce ... was charged with going around the province to speak with administrators, teachers, parents, and students about bullying in schools. And when they produced their report, the report clearly stated that the most prevalent form of bullying going on in schools in British Columbia was homophobic bullying, that they had heard about it over and over and over again. Wherever they went and whomever they spoke to, they heard about the high incidence of homophobic bullying.

When that taskforce came out with its seven recommendations about what the Ministry of Education should do about bullying in schools, not one of those recommendations addressed homophobic bullying.

Peter described how fear could be used to misinform and to secure large numbers of parents in opposition to LGBTQ curriculum change and cultural change in the classroom generally:

You misinform them about what the subject is, then you can mislead them, then you just bring them in like cattle. Because they do what they're told. The majority of them have no idea what this is about. But they're told to do it anyway because they just follow. It's a vocal minority. And quite honestly, some of the comments out of ministry staff endorse that as well. They're sort of quite fed up with this small minority giving the impression that they represent the majority [and] making a lot of noise.

Peter told me that in his experience, people of faith were both "positive and negative" about homosexuality. Murray Corren assessed interactions with religious communities and their responses to homosexuality in this way: "Any religious community, be it Christian, be it Muslim, be it the Sikh community, be it Judaism, we have seen people on both sides of the issue. Unfortunately, those who *object* are the most vocal."

Students and teachers point to religious beliefs as a potentially greater threat to personal safety and self-realization than physical bullying. Sian, in Grade 11 at Brookwood, describes the problem that religious beliefs pose to implementing a LGBTQ-inclusive curriculum:

Kids were just not receptive and I think religion was a big part of that. Who knows? Maybe you're getting through to some people, I am sure you are, but in terms of changing the culture that we were talking about before, I think it's too late for most of them. Not for kids in Grade 1 and 2 but for most of these ones ... It's not worth it to try to educate these people on the subject because you're not gonna be able to get through their minds – because there's always the religious barriers. And that's what's so frustrating. Sure, maybe, you can deal with verbal insults or even physical bullying – I mean you can punish them, you can even have clubs like Out of the Closet or stuff in sex ed or whatever – but how do you *get at* what these kinds of people are thinking when they're cloaked in their religion?

The resulting general climate of many of these schools pushes LGBTQ students to the fringes. Sian says, "I'm not intertwined in this school in depth and I don't want to be."

Silver is "a self-identified gender fuck" in Grade 11 at Triangle. She describes herself as "queer, not lesbian." She has been at Triangle for three years and is officially "in transition" back to another high school. By the time I speak with her, I have heard a lot of pessimism from LGBTQ students and others about breaking through the "religious barriers" that Sian identifies and that so many others agree are impeding the effectiveness of equity policies and transformational efforts. Silver tells me about another Toronto school she attended before coming to Triangle:

I know for a fact that a lot of the teachers there are quite homophobic, whether it's in a subtle way or in a just outright way. And I know that if a student complained that there would be like some kind of, "Oh we'll investigate it." Because they have to ... And they'd bring the teacher in and be like, "Yeah, we had a complaint from this student. So just don't say stuff like that anymore." But I guarantee you that they don't actually – that they would never actually do anything about something like that because adhering to their religion is more important than adhering to bullying policies.

Silver blames a lot of her problems at her previous school on the religion teacher:

I left because I was getting really, really threatening emails. I only told two people that I was queer inside, and I'm not sure how it was found out. But I was receiving really, really threatening emails from anonymous hotmail accounts like "dykehater520" or accounts people would make up specifically to send email to me. And I was having things written on my locker like "fat dyke," "smelly dyke." All that sort of stuff. And the religion teacher I had the year before, we had an entire day of school dedicated to how if the Pope was in charge, queer people would not be allowed to come out because it makes everyone uncomfortable. So even that was kind of like this is not the atmosphere I want to flourish in. Our religion teacher was very – she didn't like the idea of dyke – she didn't like the idea of pride pretty much ... So it was not the greatest place.

Noel, also at Triangle, laughs out loud when I ask him what role religion plays, if any, in the lives of students at his previous school.

It's like there's a little religious book they all read and carry around with them, with a little paragraph saying about how if you were a gay person, it's against God to be gay. That God created man to reproduce and continue the line of mankind. If you are a gay person and you are attracted to someone of the same sex, you could not do that and therefore you had a different agenda than straight people. Same sex is bad because you can't procreate. Which, of course, is stupid, because we could if we wanted to and a lot do.

Bruce, a teacher at a north Toronto school, talks about the role of religion in the lives of students:

It's amazing to me. I'm forty-seven and I cannot remember religion being this big a part of *my* life or in the lives of my friends when *I* was in high school. And I was a religious teenager. But it's there now and it definitely leads to a disconnect between what the policies are trying to do in terms of equity and how students experience school carrying their religious beliefs with them.

Len at Trimble Collegiate is typically succinct in describing how religion is a force that LGBTQ students and their allies must inevitably face head on:

> Religion valorizes heteronormativity and condemns queers. There's not much mystery or more to it. People who practise religion stop their thinking there. Can you call that thinking? Religion rejects queers when what it needs to do is embrace us and find a place for us in the church. I'd start with acknowledging that the priest is quite possibly queer himself.

There is an obvious link between religious beliefs of students and what they hear and learn at home. Is it possible for parents to be part of a solution?

Len not only is an older, confident student but also has experience working with community organizations. He says, "Parents are more often part of the problem, as it is, I think. They *could* be part of the solution."

Silver feels very strongly that parents are "responsible" for "queer oppression": "I think that schools are scared of parents and they take their lead from parents ... I don't think a lot of teachers or schools want to deal with what the parents will think of them. So the schools ignore [them]." According to Silver, who is white, schools are influenced by the bigotry espoused by parents who hold religious views or "romantic" views of how "they want their families to be." She tries to articulate the association between religious views and how families view themselves and their members:

> First of all, there's a tremendous number of immigrants in a lot of schools from countries where you get killed if you're a homosexual. Very negative. A lot of West Indians are unbelievable. East Indians tend to be unbelievable, Arabs. They're very homophobic and they trace it to their religion and blah, blah, blah. And Jamaicans. They're the worst, I would say, in terms of homophobia. Unbelievable. But it's not just religion, it's how these parents think about what kind of kids they've given birth to or raised and what it says about them.

Am I Safe Here?

Once entrenched, homophobia and the religious discourse that often fuels it are difficult to tackle. Inclusive education is time and again pointed to as the answer. As Trista, the Grade 11 transgender student at Triangle, puts it,

> When you're going to a mainstream high school, not only do you have to worry about your credits, but you also have to worry about your peers, like, and in being in the pecking order ... These are power-tripping teenagers, armed with religion, being defined by their religion, trying to define you. Never mind trying to find our place in society – their attitude is, "We'll tell you what it is." And what it is is heterosexist and religious-based. And forget about any LGBTQ content in the curriculum. You're going up against God, for God's sake.

Rule 3: If I Call You a Fag, Then That Means I'm Not One

Diana Goundrey deals with a lot of students in the guidance office. She says, "If a boy calls another boy a fag, he's not just defining 'the fag,' he's defining himself as straight."

Azmi Jubran is adamant that the boys and girls who bullied him were making statements about themselves as much as about him. Even though Jubran is not gay, making homophobic comments about his identity was a means for his victimizers to define themselves as "non-gay." For five years, from 1993 through 1998, Azmi attended Handsworth Secondary School in North Vancouver, where he was repeatedly assaulted, verbally and physically. He was subjected to homophobic epithets, spat at and urinated on, and kicked and punched by male and female students. As a result of defending himself during one of these assaults, Azmi faced criminal charges, of which he was eventually acquitted.

Emboldened by his experience with the criminal court, and before he graduated from high school, Azmi filed a human rights complaint alleging that he was being discriminated against on the grounds of sexual orientation. The basis of his complaint was that the Board of School Trustees was accountable for his treatment during high school because its members failed to provide an educational environment free of discriminatory harassment.[2] Azmi had been marked as "queer," even though he is not gay. Azmi suffered the day-to-day social consequences of being a targeted LGBTQ person without actually being gay.

But students often harass and mark other students as "queer" less because they believe or even assume someone else to be gay and more because doing so helps to declare and corroborate their own heterosexuality.

The forces behind Rule 2 and Rule 3 are related. Trista at Triangle is convinced that students commit wilful acts against LGBTQ students to police the borders of a "box," which most students want to stay firmly within, mostly for religious reasons. For her, this sort of oppression is therefore like religious beliefs, deep-rooted. As a result, she advocates for LGBTQ-inclusive education in the earliest grades:

> You will maybe change some of it, now, today, but only by starting early can you start to change things for tomorrow. You need education, you need to start early. I don't see any other way. It's too late for my situation. Religion got to them first and they're acting out of reflex.
>
> I know what these kids bring with them from home. I used to dress up as a kid, and if I heard my parents coming, I'd hide in my wardrobe. They were super religious and I think they're worse now. I think they'd be happier now if I had gotten trapped in my wardrobe and never came out. Sorry, too late.

Counteracting the Rules

Brent, a Grade 12 student at progressive Burton School, makes an observation that picks up on Trista's point about the interplay of religious beliefs and peer influences. He is alert to the ways that students with strong religious beliefs and negative feelings about LGBTQ students can sway others:

> Let's say you're a religious freak who hates gays. Or not even a freak, but that's still why you hate us. Well, you can influence other students because

Am I Safe Here?

the opinion most students care about is [that of] other students. More so than parents or teachers.

A lot of people are brainwashed very early by their parents. Generally, this is from religion, specifically Muslim students, in my experience. They're taught very early on that homosexuality is wrong. If they show any signs of it, they will be ostracized [by] their family and it's scary. I have a friend who is openly bisexual and Muslim, and it's a big deal. So that religious student comes to school, hates queers, and their friends pick up on it because they want to be friends with that person. You just get this whole atmosphere of hate and intolerance, bullying and fear. It's really complicated, actually.

Diana Goundrey conveys to me the challenge of creating safe and inclusive schools or engaging in inclusive education practices in the face of religious opposition: "You can't argue with somebody who says their religion justified discrimination against gay kids – it precludes any kind of an argument when someone says, 'Well, that's just my religion. That's what God said, and that's it.' Where are you going to go with that? You can't go anywhere with that."

Not everyone sees parents as the centre of the problems presented by religious beliefs. Diana doesn't. Although hers is a comparatively rare experience, she has encountered no interference from parents. She explains,

I don't think it's necessarily reinforced at home always. I think it's just the kids. We never get parents complaining about it – when I showed [the film] *Billy Elliot* [2000], I had a boy who was extremely upset about it. Threatened to beat me up over it[,] actually. A whole incident came out of it at this school. I never got a phone call from his parents. His parents didn't have a problem with it. He did.

He was kicked out – he was moved out of the school. But yeah, that extreme Christian, born-again Christian – we had a couple of teachers who were like that here who were saying some pretty scary things to kids ... They'll say, "Well, love the person, hate the action," or whatever. And it's like, "What are you saying?"

Diana, Sian, Len, and many of the others who speak to me agree that inclusive education stressing equity and social justice is the best means to counter the aggressively normative dictates of religious beliefs.

In Len's view, parents' morals are usually at odds with the need to educate students about equity and diversity. Len acknowledges that for parents and for many administrators in schools who must deal with practical difficulties, this obstacle to education is difficult to grasp:

> At the start, I would focus most on keeping the parents who are problems away. And letting them know that they don't actually have the right to interfere in equity education ... Because sometimes you'll have parents pulling students out of workshops and out of classes where they're going to be doing anti-homophobia education. At least in ... Toronto ..., that's absolutely not allowed ...
>
> But they try and often it is because of religion. It's usually either religious or moral reasons, which really means the same thing even if people don't know it – usually they're tied together. Eventually, I mean, it's certainly to be hoped that parents can play a role in educating for equity and for diversity. But I'd rather see school boards focusing their resources and their time on the student and staff first.

Silver tells me about the personal circumstances that drove her to transfer to Triangle:

> My mother was one of the first people that I told I was queer, and I sure wish I hadn't because she took it upon herself to tell every single member of both my mother's and my father's side of the family and then to lock me up when they were all appalled.
>
> First, she put me on a very, very high level of prescription medications, and I wasn't even able to stay awake during class. And I ended up being taken to a psych ward for two to three weeks because of the drugs. I don't even remember how many days I was there.
>
> And because I was gone for so long, one of the guidance counsellors actually went to my mom and said, "Do you think she's coming back or should we take her off the records?" And my mom's like, "Well, she probably won't come back. She's sick, so she's probably going to find another

Am I Safe Here?

school, especially with what's happened here, so keep her on record just so it says she's attending school, but there's a good chance she's not coming back." So my mother saw me as sick, so she made me sick, but it was a kind of sick she could talk about. Better to be a drug addict than a queer.

I found out later that what my mother did was illegal. But there's the law – and then there's what my mother says.

Sian at Brookwood Collegiate talks of the anti-snitch culture, religious beliefs, and the various ways that these influences complicate the positive effects of equity policies:

> There's only one way to "penetrate youth culture," as we were calling it. Education is the answer, but it's too late for my generation. We need to be working on the kids in kindergarten. They have to have some actual books that aren't all about [Roald Dahl's] *James and the Giant Peach* [1961] because I don't fucking care about *James and the Giant Peach*. I want to know queers ...
>
> If people were exposed to queers like me, then I wouldn't get as many dirty looks. If people were exposed to queers, then we would love them more. And religious reasons, ugh. People can say that their religion doesn't believe in this, but we can say, "Well, we believe in no hatred, so don't bring your hatred in this school and call it religion" – because they can have their religions and they can believe in that, but that doesn't mean that they have to act upon being hateful, that's unnecessary ...
>
> They're going to know me and be friends with me because for all their lives it's been normal that I'm there. But it's not like that right now.

Peter Corren and Murray Corren were keen believers that the reformation of schools requires an educative response reflected in the curriculum as well as a component that addresses the heteronormative culture in the unofficial spaces of schools. Murray Corren said,

> By the time those kids reach Grades 3 or 4, they've heard in the playground, outside the classroom, the homophobic insults, they've seen it in the media, in the general school culture, and many of them have heard homophobic stuff at home, so by the time they get to Grades 3 and 4,

they start to realize – they've gotten enough of the negative messages to tell them – there must be something wrong ...

If you want to insult and hurt somebody's feelings, that's a good epithet to use [and] if you happen to think you might be gay or lesbian, you are going to shut down and remain invisible ...

Then when they hit middle school or junior high school and the hormones are kicking in, then the verbal abuse can start to manifest itself in physical violence. And then when they get into high school, queer kids or those who were perceived to be queer, their lives [are] unbearable to the point where many of them [can] just no longer tolerate being in such a toxic environment, that they simply leave school.

Trista at Triangle expresses a similar frustration:

For straight students, when they think of queers, in their mind, they're just already programmed to say that it's wrong and to condemn it. Bullying is one step away from that. And that usually comes from very small boxes that they live in – let's call that religiously motivated, even indirectly, from their families – and it bothers them when they see some-body like me outside that box. So they bully, they threaten, they do whatever ... I had my hair cut about six times at my other school, forcibly, sitting in class, on the bus, they would just jump me and cut my hair with scissors. Boys and girls both did that to me ... So that's what you learn outside of just getting an education.

These three rules reflect the realities governing the experience of going to school for LGBTQ students. They reflect the real difficulties that are in place in schools, which must first be overcome if LGBTQ students are to receive equal access to education in schools. How do we do that? We have seen so far that law and policy must include a trans-formative educational approach.

Formal law is only one structure that can be a factor for sexual-minority youth accessing social justice. Religion, race, gender, and peer pressures are the structures behind law that also affect their access.

The last word on these three rules goes to Dalton at Brookwood Collegiate: "So you need to educate people ... That, of course, is connected to having queers at dances, less of a normative culture represented all around the school."

"The Gender Box"

Teacher Sharon Dominick at Sylvia Avenue uses an exercise she calls "The Gender Box" to illustrate the truth of all three rules and the need for transformative educational curriculum. "The Gender Box," as Sharon presents it to her class, is a hybrid of gender-inventory exercises initially developed by the Oakland Men's Project in the 1980s. Since that time, the exercise has been adapted by many groups and shaped in different ways. Sharon Dominick has her own version of it.

The students know the exercise as "Act Like a Man" and "Act Like a Lady." Sharon divides the class into two groups – boys and girls. She asks the boys to make a list of all the traits or qualities that, in their view, are characteristic of what it means to "act like a man" in our culture. She asks the girls to make a list of traits that inform our culture's idea of what it means to "act like a lady." The intention is to discuss the two lists separately and in relation to one another.

Sharon asks the students to "think about the messages that you get about what it means to be a man or what it means to be a lady." She moves to the walls of her classroom and points to the collages of advertisements that cover them, images of men and women selling products – "hawking" gender. "We've talked about this. You know this. Okay, let's go."

Each of the groups writes on a Bristol board with a magic marker. At the end of the ten-minute time limit, they have generated two lists.

This is the list the boys have created:

Act Like a Man

- tough
- aggressive
- competitive
- built
- be a pimp

- sporty
- fearless
- short hair
- baggy clothes
- clean/scruffy

- sit with legs open
- independent
- takes care of family
- provider
- protector

- humour
- don't wear girl colours
- works out
- slang
- drink beer
- an get really drunk
- physical fighting
- barbeque
- nice watch
- suits/ties
- mook
- cannot wear purple
- handy-man
- cannot act girly
- messy handwriting
- men are richer than women
- don't wear tight undies
- groomed hair
- take control of a stressful situation
- are allowed to burp
- big feet
- more about lust
- watch action flicks

And the girls have created this list:

Act Like a Lady

- clean
- sit with legs crossed
- makeup/lip gloss
- long hair
- fitting clothes
- polite
- hour glass
- smart
- emotional
- no hair on most of body
- quiet/shy
- homemakers
- clear skin
- skirts/dresses
- smell nice
- nail polish
- proper English
- manners
- takes care of herself
- dependent
- champagne, girly drinks
- don't get trashed
- know their limits
- gossiping
- if girl wears too much makeup, she looks fake or trashy-looking
- tight, fitted clothes
- must learn to cook
- not too many sex partners
- must obey parents more than men do
- wear girly colours like pink and purple
- women are more affectionate towards each other than men are, hugs and kisses, they show their emotions
- smooth skin
- let the men take power over problem
- don't burp/fart
- shorter than men
- smaller feet
- more about love
- watch sappy movies
- supportive emotionally

Policing the Borders

Sharon draws boxes around the borders of each Bristol board and then reads the lists aloud. The students hoot a few times at some of the items on the lists when their teacher says the words aloud. Sharon encourages the groups to comment on each other's list. The students do not require much encouragement – they are anxious to speak up about how they view themselves and each other.

The boys assess their own list. They decide that some of the qualities that "make a man a man" are "desirable." But they note that with being a man comes obligations and burdens that women and girls do not have to shoulder. They think this is unfair or at least different. The girls feel the same way about being a "lady." They value some of their traits but regard others as unfair distinctions between boys and girls.

Here, without any trace of Jack McFarland of *Will & Grace*, Barry speaks up. He points out that the lists contain things that both boys and girls "have" to do and traits that both "have" to possess, as well as things that are expressed in terms of negatives. There are things that boys "should not" or "do not" do and that girls "should not" or "do not" do.

Sharon writes the word "normative" on the board and points out that this is what Barry is talking about. She reminds the students that this is an issue they have discussed many times in the class's "culture jamming" exercises when looking at advertising and media images of masculinity and femininity.

A girl named Emily objects to the fact that so many of the female students began with words that characterize how a "lady" is supposed to "look." She argues for some of the traits that appear on the boys' list, such as courageous and strong, but is voted down by the other girls.

None of the boys make this observation in relation to their own process. In fact, one of the points that emerges from the students' discussion is that the boys seem to be very conscious of defining themselves in opposition to girls. The boys are what the girls are not. And the boys admit to holding this view – proudly, it seems.

The girls make it clear that this is not how they approached their list. Rather, some of the girls are very incensed by the messages society sends about being female and are glad to have the opportunity to express their outrage. However, a large number of girls do not feel this way and happily accept the standards, which they are – proudly, it seems – meeting or exceeding. And they want that known.

Another Look

Sharon leads the students through a discussion that considers each of the traits on the lists. She asks the students to consider what has been discussed. Do they now look at their lists in a "new way"?

She asks the girls, "Are there traits on your lists that you still think are desirable for girls to have, in light of our discussion, or not?" She asks the girls to circle any traits they believe are desirable only for girls.

Same thing with the boys: "Are there traits on the list that are desirable for boys? Or are they traits that *everybody* should have?"

The students return to their groups, and while they are taking a few minutes to reconsider their lists, Sharon says to me, "Of course, I'm hoping they don't circle anything." But circling has already begun.

Despite a discussion showing the boys that the girls value courage and strength and that being "emotionally supportive" is a trait that everyone can express and be appreciated for, both the boys and the girls hold to the belief that it is more desirable for boys than girls to exhibit certain traits and better for girls than boys to display others.

The boys circle the following desirable traits for boys who want to "act like a man":

- independent
- takes care of family
- clean/scruffy
- humour
- drink beer
- don't wear tight undies

Willing to concede some ground in the discussion, but unwilling to yield all of it, the boys modify "tough" on the Bristol board so that it now reads "tough (to a point)."

The girls circle these qualities:

- clean
- polite
- takes care of herself
- smart
- smell nice
- manners
- women are more affectionate towards each other
- supportive emotionally
- if girl wears too much makeup, she looks fake/trashy-looking

Here, the girls have made a modification, striking out "fake" but leaving "trashy-looking."

Sharon makes separate lists and draws a box around each one. She asks the students why they circled these particular traits.

Each of the girls who answers agrees that it is important for girls to present themselves well so that boys will be interested in them. At the same time, however, they stress that girls should not "overdo" it by being "trashy."

With the support of the other girls, Emily circled "smart." Sharon makes a note of their reasons on the blackboard.

The "F" Word ... Again

Sharon considers the boys' list and begins by asking them why wearing baggy undies is important enough to circle. Jeremiah, a black sixteen-year-old student, yells out, "So you're not called a fag!" That answer seems to meet with much approval. Sharon writes the response on the board. "I asked you and I'm writing it down," she says.

This time there is no discussion of the "F" word. Sharon explains that she wants to get them to show what is behind their thinking. She accepts their answers so that they can see the answers in front of them.

What follows is a further discussion of boys defining themselves in opposition to girls and in such a way as to make it clear to the world that they are not "homosexual." The boys who speak up indicate that it is "important" not to be perceived as "gay" or as a "fag," and they will not relent on the point.

When Sharon asks the boys how they would respond if someone described them by using words the girls circled on their list, the boys have no real problems with any of the circled items (although they laugh at "smell nice") until Sharon gets to the issue of boys being "affectionate towards each other." This would definitely be perceived as "gay" behaviour, they make clear. Some of the girls disagree with the boys on this point, but many of them do agree and believe that boys should not be as affectionate with each other as girls are with each other.

Outside the Box

Sharon asks the girls and boys to make a list of words that would be used to describe a girl who failed to act like a lady, a girl who acted outside the "box." How would people treat her?

She also asks them to make a list for a boy who operated outside the box. How would people treat him?

The girls feel that a girl who failed to act like a lady or acted outside the box would be regarded as a "slut" or a "whore" or as a "bitch" or "dirty." The boys use the same words to describe such a girl.

For a boy who failed to act like a man or who operated outside the gender box, the girls and boys again have the same words on their lists: "fag," "queer," "homo," "gay."

Sharon asks the students how they would feel if one of their friends lived outside the box, either by failing to act like a lady or to act like a man.

"I'd kick the 's' out of him," one boy says, to much laughter. The general consensus is that boys or men who choose not to act like a man are "gay." And there is not much sympathy expressed for what might happen to such a boy or man.

A few of the girls are willing to admire girls who throw social conventions aside and live more independently than society encourages "ladies" to do. But as one girl warns, "not too much."

Inside the Box

Sharon ends the exercise by asking the students to consider what price is paid when we are asked to live our lives "*inside* the box."

Am I Safe Here?

The question seems to startle the students. The boys in particular seem unwilling to acknowledge that any price is paid. It seems from the few answers the boys give to this question that the "price" of being asked to "act like a man" is not a price at all but something that should be regarded as nothing more than "natural" or "just the way it is." The boys deny that there are any pressures or constraints on them.

As Jeremiah puts it, "So long as I can drink my beer, I'm happy."

The girls seem more willing to entertain the idea of being "in a box," but that's only some of the girls, and generally, it's within strict limits.

Nature or Nurture?

Sharon began "The Gender Box" activity by asking the students whether gender is an inevitable expression of biology or a learned result. At the beginning of the exercise, the students regarded gender as a biological consequence. However, by the end, about one-third of the students, mainly girls, have conceded that gender could be a cultural consequence, but within limits.

When pressed, those students who allow for the possibility that gender can be learned tend to maintain that only certain traits can be learned and that some are always biological.

When asked to suggest which traits might be learned rather than biological, the students have difficulty doing so. As well, even when gender is viewed as a cultural consequence, the students tend to regard the "desirable" gender traits they have identified as traits to which they are "entitled" by virtue of being a boy or a girl.

A New Hope?

As I sit with Sharon Dominick on a Friday afternoon, she shows me a paper written by a student who offered it to her without a word:

> It is bad to use the term "fag" because it is not only wrong to stereotype but also to claim a group as wrong or bad. Even tho my wording was misunderstood, it should not have been used in the context of verbally bringing someone down. It is also unfair to the gay community to use a

word that they pride, to use in my benefit as a negative. No matter if it is used in a sense of homosexual negativity or not. My words were used without contemplating the safety of others so my apologies for being me and taking away your sense of security.

I ask Sharon, "Does it give you hope? Or ...?" She smiles and says, "Or is it a flower in the desert? I'll tell you the truth. I don't have a lot of hope for this school. I'm tired of it. It exhausts me. I'd still like to transfer. I want to go somewhere else. Nothing I do makes any difference here because I don't have enough support."

Sharon retrieves a folder. "Have a look. This is not a new battle. I've been fighting it for years." What I find are a pile of notes and letters. Here are three:

I don't really see how calling a rude women a cunt is bad. But it seems that it refers to women as just being some sort of object. I'm not sorry for my choice of words, but I should have released in a more dumb down way of expressing it. I realize women are not all bad and inconsiderate but it's those one or two on an off day that helped me get to the point of saying something derogatory towards women.

This expression, I feel, is Okay. I think it is OK because it is used so commonly. I suppose the matter of context it is used in is also of importance. Teenagers and pre-teens use it on a daily basis. I would not describe someone as "gay" but to describe something like a movie or place is justified. Describing someone as "gay" may be going over the limit. Thus, I feel it is OK to say "gay" depending on the context. Just because it is already commonly used.

I think that using the phrase "that's so gay" is okay to use as long as you are not offending anyone when you are saying it. In most cases someone would seriously be offended. Therefore it should not be said, and only thought of in the very least because the term is used incorrectly and offends people.

Am I Safe Here?

Some weeks later, when I am at Triangle, I mention "The Gender Box" exercise to Trista, the transgender student I have met and talked with on several occasions. She says,

> Well, gender to a lot of people is assigned at birth. I was born a male and to them that means being masculine. If I call you a fag, then that means I'm not one, doesn't it? And that affects, of course, the position of women, too. I think homosexuality is something to be hidden in places like North Bay, where I come from, because it's really the fact that it makes people uncomfortable about moving outside of what your particular gender is supposed to be about.

Trista sums up the "gender box" in which she lived her life for seventeen years:

> There wasn't one day that I could get by without having to be stoned just to deal with the shit that people put me through just because I wanted to move outside the box that you were talking about. Just awful, horrible stuff. They cut my hair, they called me names, they put a knife to my throat. But I never cried. I didn't have emotions. I pulled away and told myself it would all be over and I'd leave as soon as I possibly could. As soon as I got the chance, I was going to leave North Bay. And I did.

I do not wish to end Trista's story on a mournful note. By her own description, Trista is happy now at Triangle – she believes she is thriving *because* of Triangle:

> Triangle is an excellent idea. I think they should have one in every major city, only because, in this way, queer people, queer youth, could have a safe place to go and educate themselves and not have to deal with the crap that I went through and a lot of the other students went through. And this is why a lot of the students are here. They couldn't deal with mainstream high school. The religious crap, the way the jocks are, their girlfriends, all of it. And that gender box, yeah, all of it.

Sharon shows me a letter from a former student of hers that she received several years after the events described in the letter:

Dear Miss Sharon Dominick,

Over the years, you have been a great teacher and someone I can depend on. Personally speaking, if there is an award for best teacher in the world, I think you would be a perfect candidate for it. Not only do you make the time to help your students, but you also take the time to talk to them as a friend, not just a teacher. And that is how I think every teacher should be. Many teachers can learn a thing or two from you ...

This letter is a thank you for all the times you have been there to help me when I needed it the most. Especially in the tenth grade with all the problems I had being called the F word and when I got suspended. You were very supportive, and you still are. If it was not for what you did for me about my suspension, I would not have had someone in this school I could trust and seek advice from.

I hope you never go to another school. That school would never be the same without you there, and all of your cool posters and ads and pictures!!

It's a joy just walking by and seeing what new things you have put up to help the students "culture jam" and get out of the "gender box."

I hope to see you again. Thank you.

Sincerely,
Doug

Summing Up

Despite the effects of a normative youth culture that prizes fitting in and punishing "snitching" – a culture whose "rules" must be taken into account when considering effective laws, policies, and programs aimed at ensuring equity and safe schools for LGBTQ students – the actions of individuals "on the ground," especially teachers like Sharon, do help to counter these influences. Transformative change needs to happen in all schools. Social justice should be for all students, not just for a fortunate few who have teachers like Sharon Dominick.

This chapter has underscored and expanded on a point made throughout this book: solutions lie in efforts and influences embedded in the official curriculum and other inclusive education practices, such as the formation of GSAs. The importance of such responses is highlighted by the presence of other influences and factors in schools that work to counter the idea of safety as equity and inclusiveness.

The three factors highlighted in this chapter – the rules that govern school culture – must be considered when developing new approaches to school safety. The anti-snitch culture in schools, the religious beliefs and practices that influence student and parental attitudes and behaviours, and the pressure of internalized gender codes, or appropriate behaviours for girls and boys, are powerful dynamics that cannot be ignored.

These forces need to be offset by concerted curricular efforts in each school, from the early grades through Grade 12, to recognize, affirm, celebrate, and include each school's LGBTQ citizens. Key to overcoming fears of undertaking this work in the early grades is the realization that bullying and harassment are more than just kids being kids and that victimization has long-term consequences for those who are victimized, as well as making the environment toxic for everyone else. Thorough teacher training, support, and resources are vital.

It is important for administrators and educators to regard LGBTQ rights as human rights established in law. The law provides support and justification for LGBTQ-inclusive education. The grounds, then, for equitable, inclusive education are to be found not in religious history, dogma, or practices but in human rights legislation and in policies rooted in human rights that support and implement safe schools as equitable and inclusive places for LGBTQ students.

What Needs to Be Done

- The pervasiveness of anti-snitch culture, religious influences, and strongly held attitudes of appropriate gender behaviour that many students demonstrate underscores that inclusive education must begin in the early grades and continue throughout the K–12 system.

- The negative effects of the anti-snitch culture, in general, are a strong argument in favour of the curriculum as a place where LGBTQ lives and realities must be presented and reinforced.
- The fact that there are many in the school environment (and at home) who hold strong religious beliefs and convictions suggests two factors that must be considered at all times in developing safe, equitable, and inclusive schools for LGBTQ students:

  ⋏ First, LGBTQ rights must be understood to constitute human rights, notably the right of LGBTQ students to go to school in safety, with *safety* defined to include equity and inclusiveness.
  ⋏ Second, to counter the negative view of LGBTQ students and their lives often held by those espousing religious beliefs and dogma, the curriculum must provide a different view – a positive, celebratory depiction of LGBTQ realities and lives in which LGBTQ students and/or the LGBTQ parents of students are embraced.

- Gender codes must be counterbalanced by a curriculum that permits students to move from within the confines of a gender box to a freer sense of gender. Strict notions of what is appropriate gender behaviour inform homophobia, heterosexism, and the heterormativity of schools.
- The need to reorganize school culture should be regarded by administrators not as an indicator of an unhealthy, unsettled school, where trouble is brewing, but as an indicator of a school that considers and is addressing the needs of all of its students.

5

What Now?

What will they do when they read this? What would
the ramifications for school policy be if they listened to
students?

– Ryan, Grade 9 student, Toronto

An Inclusive Definition of *Safety*

The stories and reflections in this book show that LGBTQ students define
safety much more broadly, in most cases, than do their own schools. They
believe that *safety* has to be defined in a way that makes room for a significant impact on the school culture in general, not just defined as
something that is pursued in response to incidents of violence after they
happen. As Lazy Daisy says, "It's about changing the attitude, the root
of the problem, not just doing something about an isolated incident."
Students and their allies support transformative strategies in the education system and curriculum.

Many students view heteronormativity as more immediately threatening to their personal identities than the fear of physical or verbal harassment. Again, Lazy Daisy aptly summarizes the situation: "Safety for
queer kids is ... not just about bullying, I mean, in a physical way. We're
bullied by just the culture we're in." However, these students acknowledge
that for many, if not most, students, including students in smaller cities

and in rural settings, concerns about physical and verbal violence are significant and likely more immediate.

Students and their teachers offer a critique of current approaches to safety – including the security guards, surveillance cameras, and ID tags – by pointing to the need to conceptualize safety in terms of *doing equity* or, beyond that, as a matter of social justice. Although all of the students believe that safety should include equity, the majority of students say their schools do not conceptualize safety in this way. For most of these students, the approach to safety at their own schools displays a "fortress mentality" by emphasizing security in response to a culture of fear rather than focusing on equity. There is often a disconnect between how the students conceive of safety and how they experience safety from day to day "on the ground."

Both students and teachers made a number of suggestions for improvement that emphasize equity and position safety alongside human rights principles. These are summarized at the end of each chapter and are also revisited below. Students and teachers conceive of safety policies not only as responding to injustices, like complaint- and incident-based systems do, but also, and more importantly, as being proactive about achieving social justice for LGBTQ students.

Getting There

Well, a policy is only as good as its implementation
and, anyway, I think it's important to get the staff aware
of the problem and that there's a need for change.
That's equally important [as] just having an anti-
harassment policy.

– *Terrence, Grade 12 student*

I think you really have to crack down on practically
everything, so I think, yeah, they need to focus more on
educating people. Because you know, like I said before,
everybody has an extreme problem with boys wearing

nail polish or eyeliner or whatever. I feel like everybody has a right to a safe space at school, a legal right,
right? But, like, I never really knew how to do anything
about it because normally, if you speak up, it makes
things worse.

– Ryan, Grade 9 student

The proposals that are ultimately favoured by the students can be summarized as follows, representing the major themes that have emerged
throughout this book.

1. *It is important to conceive of safety broadly and to view safety in terms
    of equity and inclusiveness.*

Discussions of "safe schools" have for years positioned the issues of
bullying and school safety as separate from the issues of equity and
social justice. The discussions have often been mired in conversations
about school violence and zero-tolerance policies. Policy approaches
that emphasize the management and governance of conduct fail to
engage with the multiple ways that bullying props up the normative
cultural values and privilege at the root of the problem.

The interviews featured in this book support a policy approach
in which students are not viewed as the source of the threat to school
safety. Imagine if retail stores treated their customers as though each
one was a shoplifter – this is how some students feel in their own
schools. Instead, the LGBTQ students I have spoken with identify
the larger heteronormative climate of schools as often the greatest
source of their oppression and exclusion from feeling safe, recognized,
and celebrated.

Students believe that safety policies and interpretations of policies should be framed in terms of equity and inclusiveness, but most
also report that their own schools pursue safety in terms of security,
emphasizing responsiveness to individual incidents of bullying,
surveillance, student IDs, cameras, and a general herding and controlling of the student population.

This incongruity leads to the conviction that mandated curricular content is necessary in order to change the school culture. Inclusive responses, both in the official space of the curriculum and in unofficial spaces like hallways and schoolyards, can change the depiction of LGBTQ students as "other," countering the denial of their full citizenship in schools. Many students have spoken to me at length about the distinction between reactive, disciplinary policies and proactive, educative responses. Cal, from Elizabeth Coyt Alternative School, puts it this way:

> So if a high school had strictly anti-harassment policies, and they said, "You can't say *fag* and you can't beat people up because they're gay," would that be enough? It would not be enough. I think it would be a good start. But I think that a lot of stuff is needed as far as educating people. So I do think there needs to be more education. I think stopping the harassment is the first step, but ...

Cal, of course, is right. Teachers and principals have a common law, and in some provinces a statutory duty, to ensure the safety of students in their care. Administrators can find support in law for pursuing safety in terms of equity and human rights. Human rights legislation in all provinces guarantees that all students have a right to receive education free of discrimination. Some provinces – Ontario, Manitoba, and Alberta – have passed legislation that guarantees students the right to form gay-straight alliances (GSAs) in their schools and the right to call them GSAs. The LGBTQ students, and their allies, in this book argue that their safety must be conceptualized broadly if their safety is to be meaningful and effective.

2. *Mandated curriculum changes that reflect LGBTQ realities and LGBTQ lives must be implemented, commencing in the early grades.*

The first step is for LGBTQ students to see themselves reflected in all aspects of school culture. LGBTQ students are already discussed and defined at all sites of every school – unofficially. In locker rooms, sports fields, hallways, and cafeterias, and even in classrooms behind the teacher's back (or sometimes by teachers), LGBTQ students are openly derided and made fun of. If LGBTQ students are being discussed in the unofficial spaces of schools, they must be recognized and appreciated in the official spaces of schools. This unofficial curriculum transmits social meanings and promotes cultural outcomes through schooling practices and activities that occur within schools.

There is an enormous need, then, for LGBTQ lives and realities to be supported by official curriculum, and this inclusiveness must be mandatory. Optional approaches will not work because teachers will not, generally, incorporate the material into their courses due to a lack of resources, training, or support. Mandatory inclusion should not be presented as a feature of a larger course on social issues or problems. Instead, the school needs to recognize and embrace LGBTQ students and the LGBTQ parents of students in all aspects of school culture – in the official curriculum and in extracurricular pursuits and social activities. Cal, at the very progressive Elizabeth Coyt Alternative School, describes what actually happens at most other schools: "If they deal with these things at all, queer issues at all, I think there might be, like, a handout! It's really just not talked about, kind of like a taboo topic. But here, we don't question it. There's queer curriculum and people everywhere. We're always doing things. We work very differently from other schools."

LGBTQ youth in most schools are compelled to negotiate the hidden curriculum of heteronormativity in the classroom, in the hallways, and even outside of school space when they communicate with their peers – and, sometimes, with their families – about their experiences at school. As Dalton, a Grade 12 student, puts it, "Heteronormativity sort of skews all the day-to-day things and makes life in schools pretty heterosexist."

That there is surveillance of sexuality and reinforcement of heteronormative codes of behaviour in secondary schools should not be startling. The profound impact of these processes on LGBTQ students also speaks to the need to begin curricular and other responses in the early grades, when these processes begin. Sam, a Grade 12 student at Grosvenor Secondary School, remembers something he experienced in Grade 6:

When I was in Grade 6, two or three guys from my grade, they decided to make a website about me. About all the things that I did every day. All the things that they found weird, strange, gay, whatever. I remember what was especially hurtful was that they had a guest book that anybody could comment on. I remember these people commenting, as well as a group of girls from a different school, commenting on what I did every day. It was hurtful. It was embarrassing.

The cultural truth that such conduct occurs is the answer to those who wrongly assert that students in early grades are "too young" to be exposed to these topics – they are already being exposed to them and, in many cases, are already participating in such discussions and performing such practices.

3.   *Curriculum changes must also examine heterosexual privilege. LGBTQ students should not be perceived as the problem.*

Mandated curriculum change must also implicate the privilege and social rank of heterosexual students. LGBTQ content in the curriculum should not be merely "inclusive," leaving privilege unchallenged. Curriculum must examine the social construction of the sexuality and gender of all students in order to contest cultural hierarchies rather than sustaining a normative order of gender and sexuality, as well as other privileges. Trista, the Grade 11 transgender student at Triangle, tells me about "walking the gender and sexuality line" at her middle school:

> In no uncertain terms, my old school was all about status quo for gender and sexuality. Our school told us that we weren't allowed to promote homosexuality by having a GSA and that if you're flamboyant, it was the reason why you're being, you know, verbally or physically harassed. When they used to grab me and cut my hair, the school said, "It's because you're too flamboyant, you're not normal."

Am I Safe Here?

Merely acknowledging LGBTQ students does little to remove their status as "other" within the school and to erase the line between normal and different. Instead, the position of LGBTQ persons needs to be taught and understood both in terms of the cultural reasons for the bullying of this group and in terms of their social position historically in order to understand and challenge the normative social hierarchies. Otherwise, the heteronormativity of schools will be maintained, and LGBTQ students will continue to feel disconnected, excluded, or unrecognized. Their continued (official) invisibility and exclusion are as much a source of harassment and oppression of LGBTQ students as bullying, and in many cases, more so.

Programs and intervention strategies that are designed merely to address homophobia offer limited solutions. They uphold the perspective of violence against LGBTQ students that, first, views violence as implicating only individuals, not the larger culture, and second, limits notions of violence to physical violence. Equally, such programs may focus upon the LGBTQ student as "other" and do little else to address additional ways that oppression is expressed in schools through race, class, and so on.

For many students, heteronormativity is what they consider "natural," "normal," and "the way things are." However, all citizens of the school need to understand how heteronormativity is deployed in schools, how it pervades school space, and how it is perceived by many LGBTQ students as threatening to their own identity. Echoing many of the students I have spoken with, Trista tells me about the dominating culture of the school she attended before Triangle:

> Gender variance wasn't something that sits very well with most schools, not being normal. I didn't want to be visible. I was stoned most of the time, to stop it from affecting me. That's how I kept myself going.

4. *Early-career teacher training and workshops must be provided so that teachers feel the support of their colleagues and administrators, and they must have the resources to promote equity.*

For equity and inclusive education to become the mandate of school boards and school districts, money must be found and teacher training and professional development must be implemented. As it is, there is insufficient support for teachers who engage or want to engage in these practices. There are too few teachers working to develop a culture of equity and inclusion. Lorna Gillespie, the teacher who permits her students to write on the walls, expresses her frustration over the lack of a whole-school, corner-to-corner, educational approach:

> I nail students every time they do the "gay" thing and then it's, "Oh sorry, Miss" – so they know. But I don't think other teachers typically nail them, usually not in the hall and not even in their class. So many teachers don't think it matters. Or they say to me that students don't really mean anything when they say "that's so gay." The word has changed now, right? That's what the kids say, too. Want to let themselves off the hook. Or the teachers are tired. It does get exhausting being a one-man band. There are times when even I let it go. At the end of the day, some kid I don't know, right behind me, says "that's so gay" in conversation, I'm not gonna get into a big stink about it. I go into a big stink about it in my class where I can actually talk to them about it.

Cultural transformation is not going to be achieved ad hoc by a few teachers trying to make their classrooms safe, equitable, and inclusive. A whole-school approach is needed in which every teacher is encouraged and supported by administrators in all classrooms of the school. Teachers require training, resources, and support to make this happen. And that begins with early-career teacher training that not only includes but also *emphasizes* social justice concerns in the classroom. In order to achieve what is needed for LGBTQ students to feel safe based on how they define *safety* – that is, in order to do equity and create inclusive schools in which these students feel connected – teachers must receive the training and resources they need, and they, too, must feel safe and supported.

Too many teachers do not see the safety concerns of LGBTQ youth as part of their job; too many lack time. Many courageous teachers have led the charge, and many efforts have been undertaken through student-led activism. But there needs to be more systemic effort, as well as general support from administrators throughout the careers of teachers. Cultural transformation should not be carried out on the backs of some teachers and students who are creating the odd oasis in the vast wasteland of schools, and in fact, such corner-to-corner reformation of schools is not possible without general support.

The students and teachers featured in this book agree that, although the legislature and policy makers may face significant challenges in drafting reform that acknowledges and protects LGBTQ students in these ways, nothing less than a transformational process is needed.

There is little doubt that the work being undertaken now by students and teachers is complicated, political, and long-term. Also, the work may seem more incremental some days than others. These are not reasons not to begin now.

Equity Is for All Teachers, Including the Math Teacher

Many teachers will ask, "What does equity or inclusive education have to do with what I teach?" Math, geography, and physics, for example, may not, on their face, appear to give rise to opportunities to include inclusive education content or to achieve equity in their particular lesson plan or curriculum. That is not so. Teachers use examples to illustrate. And most examples are unintentionally heteronormative, as this book has shown most of the school culture to be.

A math problem, no matter how innocuous, and with no apparent intention to do so, can exclude LGBTQ students or students whose parents are gay. Over time, the snowball effect of merely not saying anything about them at all is to remind them, and everyone else, that LGBTQ folks don't really count.

A blackboard example like *Ted and his parents, Mr. and Mrs. Jones, travelled 120 kilometres on a four-day journey. How many kilometres on average did they travel each day?* could easily become *Ted and his parents, Mr. Jones and Mr. Smith.*

Geography could certainly include how Pride is celebrated in different countries.

There are other, better ways to make the curriculum more inclusive, but these examples illustrate the point. And it is an incredibly important point to understand and embrace. No one would argue that this simple math question constitutes bullying, but for LGBTQ students, the aggressively normal, wall-to-wall heterosexuality of schools is negating and suffocating. They do not see themselves reflected anywhere in the school. This is the point that so many of the people in this book make, arguing for the kind of transformation that schools must undergo.

The heteronormativity that governs most schools and normalizes the position of so-called straight kids means that the information that heterosexual students receive about LGBTQ youth is received by them in their normative positions. To address this circumstance, students recommend a mandated curriculum that includes a study of the social construction of sexuality and gender so that repetitions of normalcy are not sustained.

For LGBTQ students, elementary schools and the middle grades are among the most hurtful spaces in our school system. The reformation that must occur in schools, therefore, must begin early and with broad definitions of *safety* in mind.

The process of reorganization will be wide-ranging and complex, but each corner of the school at any given moment of the entire experience of what it means to go to school must be engaged to promote the full citizenship of LGBTQ students. It follows that the efforts to create safe, equitable, and inclusive schools for these citizens must start early – and math is taught throughout the schooling experience.

It is a job for all teachers.

I return to the question that Gabe Picard and his principal argued about: *How do we change a culture?* The stories throughout this book remind us that "something else is needed" and push us to realize that the full, robust picture of how education is delivered is implicated – from the curriculum to extracurricular activities. Student connectedness and inclusiveness in both are crucial to the elimination of the oppression, harassment, and bullying of LGBTQ students.

The curriculum must not only acknowledge the presence of its LGBTQ students and parents but must also celebrate them in the countless ways that the realities – the childhoods and families – of every other school citizen are recognized and celebrated. LGBTQ students do not just mysteriously arrive in high school – they are in school from the start, and their lives, and the lives of LGBTQ parents, must be acknowledged and celebrated from the first day all students go to school.

In addition to the curriculum, there are other influences operating in schools that must also be taken into account. Students point to peer pressures, particularly in the form of the anti-snitch culture of many schools, which has an extreme presence in some. Students, teachers, and parents also have religious beliefs that inform their positions with respect to LGBTQ persons, as well as convictions, formed over their lifetimes, as to appropriate behaviours based upon gender.

Each of these influences can work to isolate and undermine the connectedness and personal happiness of the LGBTQ student in school. But these factors also, by their very force, speak to the need for an equitable and inclusive educative component in all school years, including the early grades.

What about Your School?

The robustness of the need to pursue safety as an issue of equity and inclusiveness can be found in the stories and conversations of the students and their allies that have been presented here. The safe, equitable, and inclusive school will happen if trustees, principals, vice-principals, guidance counsellors, social workers, teachers, and other staff take up the anthem of what, for most of them, has been an outside movement.

This is the *something else* that is needed. Nothing less will do. Although there may be unique challenges in implementing reform that acknowledges and protects LGBTQ students in new ways, and although the students and their allies are very much aware that nothing less than what might be a long transformational process will bring about these changes, they also believe these are not excuses for inaction.

Doing equity, in law, has traditionally meant finding justice for individuals given the individual facts and circumstances of each case. What can this mean for LGBTQ students in the context of safe schools? We have only to listen to what they have said to imagine it.

Notes

Introduction

1 Michael Flood, "Homophobia and Masculinities among Young Men (Lessons in Becoming a Straight Man)." Presentation to teachers, O'Connell Education Centre, Canberra, April 22, 1997.

2 Bill 13, *An Act to amend the Education Act with Respect to Bullying and Other Matters*, 1st Sess., 40th Leg., Ontario, 2012 (assented to June 19, 2012), RSO 2012, c. 5; Bill 18, *The Public Schools Amendment Act (Safe and Inclusive Schools)*, 2nd Sess., 40th Leg., Manitoba, 2012 (assented to September 13, 2013), RSM 2013, c. 6.

Chapter 1: Changing the Culture

1 Isabela Varela, "New Canada Research Chair Focused on Advocating for Sexual and Gender Minority Youth," *Illuminate: Faculty of Education Magazine* (University of Alberta), November 26, 2014, http://illuminate.ualberta.ca/content/new-canada-research-chair-focused-advocating-sexual-and-gender-minority-youth.

2 Catherine Taylor and Tracey Peter, *Every Class in Every School: Final Report on the First National Climate Survey on Homophobia, Biphobia, and Transphobia in Canadian Schools* (Toronto: Egale Canada Human Rights Trust, 2011), http://egale.ca/wp-content/uploads/2011/05/EgaleFinalReport-web.pdf.

Chapter 2: How Safe Is My School?

1 Catherine Taylor, Liz Meyer, Tracey Peter, and Donn Short, *Every Teacher in Every School* (Toronto: Egale Human Rights Trust/Manitoba Teachers Society, 2015).

2 *Human Rights Code*, RSO 1990, c. H.9.

3 *Canadian Charter of Rights and Freedoms,* Part 1 of the *Constitution Act, 1982,* being Schedule B to the *Canada Act 1982* (UK), 1982, c. 11.

Chapter 3: Homophobia, Heterosexism, and Heteronormativity

1 *Youth Criminal Justice Act,* SC 2002, c. 1.
2 Jeffrey White, Anthony Grandy, and Adrienne Magidsohn of the Triangle Program, "Mission," n.d., http://schools.tdsb.on.ca/triangle/mission.html.
3 See Carol Johnson, "Heteronormative Citizenship and the Politics of Passing," *Sexualities* 5, 3 (2002): 317–36.

Chapter 4: Rules to Live By, or How to Succeed in School without Really Changing Anything

1 Obie Trice, featuring Akon, "Snitch," *Second Round's on Me,* audio CD (New York: Shady Records, 2006).
2 *Jubran v. North Vancouver School District No. 44,* 2002 BCHRT 10 at para. 3, 42 CHRR D/273.